MERLEAU-PONTY

MERLEAU-PONTY
Perception, Structure, Language
A Collection of Essays

edited by
John Sallis

HUMANITIES PRESS
ATLANTIC HIGHLANDS, N.J.

ISBN 0-391-02382-9

Reprinted from RESEARCH IN PHENOMENOLOGY 1980 Volume 10. Published in book form in the United States of America by Humanities Press, Inc. with permission of the editors.

Printed in the United States of America

Library of Congress Cataloging in Publication Data

Main entry under title:

Merleau-Ponty, perception, structure, language.

"Reprinted from Research in phenomenology, 1980, volume 10."
1. Merleau-Ponty, Maurice, 1908-1961—Addresses, essays, lectures.
2. Phenomenology—Addresses, essays, lectures. I. Merleau-Ponty, Maurice, 1908-1961.
II. Sallis, John, 1938-   . III. Research in phenomenology.
B2430.M3764M47   194   81-6799
ISBN 0-391-02382-9   AACR2

CONTENTS

Study Project on the Nature of Perception (1933)
The Nature of Perception (1934)

MAURICE MERLEAU-PONTY
Translated by Forrest Williams

Translator's Preface

On April 8, 1933, Maurice Merleau-Ponty, who was then teaching at a *lycée* in Beauvais, applied to the *Caisse National des Sciences* for a subvention, which he received, to undertake a project of study on the nature of perception. In 1934, he requested a renewal, and submitted an account, which he titled 'The Nature of Perception,'' of what he had already accomplished and of what he proposed to do next. The renewal request was not granted.

Apart from three book reviews and some remarks made at a philosophy conference, *La Structure du Comportement*, which was completed in 1938 and published in 1942, is generally considered the first evidence of Merleau-Ponty's major philosophical concerns. In a sense, that is so. However, the two earlier texts translated below, relatively short and schematic though they are, may never the less be of interest to students of Merleau-Ponty's philosophy. As can be shown, I think, by a brief analysis of their contents, Merleau-Ponty had articulated fairly clearly, some four years before the completion of *Structure*, a number of motifs that proved to be fundamental throughout his intellectual career. Naturally, his ideas were to expand and develop from 1933 to the drafts for *Le Visible et l' invisible* on which he was working at the time of his death in 1961. Therefore, it is also interesting to notice themes of his later work that were not envisaged at the outset. Professor Susanne Langer remarked in *Feeling and Form* that thinking at its best tends to develop, not by starting with the ultimate questions ("the problem of beauty," "the problem of Being," "the problem of mind," and the like), but by attacking an issue both specific and fecund. "A single problem," she wrote, "doggedly pursued to its solution, may elicit a new logical vocabulary, i.e., a new set of ideas, reaching beyond the problem itself and forcing a more negotiable conception of the whole field."[1] A brief look at these earliest of formal philosophical statements by Merleau-Ponty, with the subsequent development of his views in mind, suggests indeed that he had taken a firm grip by 1933 on a specific set of issues in the field of psychological research that were to prove philosophically fertile and that were to lead to vaster questions.

Although the concerns expressed by Merleau-Ponty in 1933-1934 clearly anticipate much of his first book (*Structure*), and some of *Phénoménologie de la Perception*, their philosophical horizon was certainly far narrower than that which he ultimately offered to modern phenomenology. Thus, although Merleau-Ponty stressed the problem of "perception of one's own body," a theme which was eventually to lead to his distinctive notion of "bodily intentionality," its real importance in his thought is apparent to us only with the advantage of hindsight. There is no hint of the "bodily reversibility" which he fastened upon more and more in his later works, where the phenomenon of the touched becoming the touching is a bodily anticipation of the reflexivity of thought. Consequently, we find also no indication of the limitations which he later placed upon intellectual reflexivity because of the limitations he experienced in the "touched-touching" state of affairs, namely, that the wonted coincidence is ever imminent yet never realized;[2] like Apollo in pursuit of Daphne, one might say. In the 1933 text, he was not yet speaking of Edmund Husserl and phenomenology, and in neither text is there any sign of the subsequent importance of the work of Martin Heidegger. Consequently, there is no apparent readiness to take on the epistemology and metaphysics of the "object" which later challenged him more and more (notably, of course, in the drafts and working notes for *Visible*). That the philosophical crisis posed by "*le Grand Objet*" was not yet evident to him was surely due in part to the more or less non-historical approach of these early statements. His eventual concern with language is not anticipated; nor can one guess the relevance to the study of perception of the arts, e.g., painting. Much less could one guess that the study of the nature of perception could lead into political and social issues, especially those surrounding Marxism and, finally, into nothing less than a new ontology.

Yet for all the great difference in range, in horizon, these texts of 1933-1934 also reveal with what maturity of mind, even before his first book, Merleau-Ponty had already defined the direction and many of the principal motifs of the succeeding 28 years of creative work. The most striking and persistent theme of his *oeuvre* was his insistence on the *philosophical* importance of the basic concept of *"Gestaltpsychologie."* We know that Merleau-Ponty had become familiar, by 1934 at least, with the thought of Aron Gurwitsch, whose 1929 article in the *Psychologische Forschung* is cited in the 1934 text. As the subtitle of the article (*'Phänomenologie der Thematik und des reinen Ich: Studien über Beziehungen von Gestalttheorie und Phänomenologie'*) clearly showed, Gurwitsch wished to call attention to the Husserlian implications of the notion of "Gestalt," terming the Gestalt psychologists' rejection of the traditional "constancy hypothesis" tantamount to a phenomenological reduction.[3] Similarly—and very likely prompted by the Gurwitsch article and Paris lectures—the 1934 statement sees profound implications in the notion of "Gestalt."[4] Already he was criticising the Gestalt psychologists for failing to live up to their own findings, a charge that he was to press vigorously a few years later in *Structure*, where he in effect accused them of running with the hares of Gestalt theory while hunting with the hounds of Cartesian dualism. Thus, what began in 1933-1934 as a specific issue in experimental psychology became for him a guiding-thread of all his philosophy. Much more than the concept which can be found neatly defined in any dictionary today, it became for him one of those indices that generate inquiry and questions to the end, rather than winding them down. He never pretended to have exhausted this notion which he placed at the center of his 1933 study project, as is tellingly shown in one of his last working notes, where he asked, "What is a Gestalt?".[5]

During the late 20's and early 30's Merleau-Ponty was faced in the academies with problems posed primarily in a Kantian or neo-Kantian fashion. But unlike such influential thinkers as Léon Brunschvicg, who concentrated chiefly on what might be called "intra-philosophical" questions, Merleau-Ponty seemed to have been moved to philosophical inquiry rather more by current contradictions which were not necessarily associated already with philosophical difficulties. (In this he was more like Henri Bergson and William James, and even Edmund Husserl, who came to philosophy through the study of mathematics.) His lifelong affinity for current issues in the wide world—viz., the artistic transformations of modern painting, the political disappointments of both East and West, the vexing "Freudian unconscious," the child psychology of Piaget and others, the American and French investigations in cultural anthropology—was already evident in 1933-1934, in his ambition to liberate empirical psychology from the grip of "Critical" philosophy. At that time—and indeed, to this day among those who are not strict behaviorists banning any reference to "mind" at all—most psychologists assumed a Kantian or neo-Kantian epistemology, according to which perceiving consists in applying intellectual interpretations to "sensations" or "sensory signs." He saw the entire "intellectualist" tradition from Descartes to Kant, however great their other differences, to be alike in misconstruing the nature of perceptual experience. Moreover, in the 1934 statement Merleau-Ponty was already hinting at the notion, fully developed in *Phénoménologie*, that the other favorite of many experimental psychologists, the philosophy of empiricism, was in no better a position: indeed, might even betray the very same misconception in a different form. He objects in the same sentence to psychologies which would make of normal perception either a "brute given" or a "construction." Later, it became clear that he believed both empiricism and Critical philosophy invented "facts" out of supposed elements and inferences for whose occurrence in perception there is no evidence. Yet another anticipation of his later writings may be found in the expressed desire to include the topics of psychopathology and developmental psychology in his study of perception. The discussion of Gelb & Goldstein's brain-injured soldier in *Phénoménologie* comes immediately to mind, as does the 1950-1951 course at the Sorbonne on the child's relations with others.[6]

Some other motifs worth noting do not all of them survive intact. Certainly the notions of perceptual distance and perceptual depth as something other than the Cartesian "width seen sideways" were to remain and become crucially important; for example, in *Phénoménologie*, in the discussion of Descartes' *Dioptrique* in *L'Oeil et l'Esprit*, and most powerfully in *Visible*, where these motifs enabled Merleau-Ponty to disclose a commingling of the visible and the invisible in a philosophy quite different from the more traditional equating of the visible with the sensory given and the invisible with the intellectually conceived. The rather definite line imagined between the phenomenological and the psychological, however, did not withstand the test of time; nor did the line between essence and fact, eidetic and inductive. In his reference in the 1934 statement to binocular vision and the disparity of retinal images, he spoke of the latter as a "condition" of vision; later, he was to question the notion of "conditions and conditioned" in terms of a "circular causality." In *Visible*, he was to return to this issue to say that these "conditions" are "not really conditions, since the images are defined as disparate only by relation to a perceptual apparatus that seeks its equilibrium in the fusion of analogous images, and hence here the 'conditioned' conditions the condition."[7]

But this step could not be taken, it seems, until the specific problem of perception addressed in 1933-1934 had turned into a clue—the richest and most suggestive clue—to nothing less than a new ontology, a theory of Being. The objections in these early texts to Critical philosophy and to empiricism as employed by psychologists had to grow into a massive confrontation with the entire tradition of abosolutised "objectivity," "Being-as-object," and its inevitable counterpart, "subjectivity." Such a confrontation also had to wait upon, and in a sense was equivalent to, a rejection of the vocabulary of "consciousness" in which Merleau-Ponty was still involved in 1933-1934, and from which he was trying to liberate himself in *Phénoménologie.*[8] What Merleau-Ponty clearly saw in 1933, these early statements reveal, was a crisis in psychology that was conspicuously evident in what was being said about perception. The sense of philosophy as we have understood it in the West, and therefore of Western culture itself, as in crisis, was still some years off. Even allowing for differences in tone due to differences in context (a formal application for a grant, a note to oneself), some measure of the trajectory from Merleau-Ponty's study project published here to the project on which he was working when he died may be gained by juxtaposing the first lines of each:

> It has seemed to me that in the present state of neurology, experimental psychology (particularly, psychopathology) and philosophy, it would be useful to take up again the problem of perception, and particularly, perception of one's own body.
> Our state of non-philosophy—The crisis has never been so radical.[9]

Acknowledgment

Although the texts translated here exist in the public domain, my work has been materially facilitated by the opportunity to translate from the French texts reproduced in Professor Theodore F. Geraets' splendid book on Merleau-Ponty's early writings, *Vers une nouvelle philosophie transcendantale: La genèse de la philosophie de Maurice Merleau-Ponty jusqu'à la Phénoménologie de la Perception* (The Hague: Martinus Nijhoff, 1971; volume 39, 'Phaenomenologica,' Centre d'Archives-Husserl), pp. 9-10, pp. 188-199. I should also like to express my thanks to Martinus Nijhoff, Publishers—without whom, it is not too much to say, so much of phenomenology would not have its wide hearing today in the philosophical *Lebenswelt*—for their gracious permission to translate from their publication.

F.W.

NOTES

[1]Susanne K. Langer, Feeling and Form (New York: Charles Scribner's Sons, 1953), p. 9.

[2]Cp. Maurice Merleau-Ponty, *The Visible and the Invisible* (Evanston, Ill.: Northwestern University Press, 1968; ed. Claude Lefort, trans. Alphonso Lingis), p. 9.

[3]Cp. Aron Gurwitsch, 'Phenomenology of Thematics and of the Pure Ego: Studies of the Relation between Gestalt Theory and Phenomenology,' in *Studies in Phenomenology and Psychology* (Evanston, Ill.: Northwestern University Press), esp. pp. 192ff.

[4]Aron Gurwitsch gave a series of lectures entitled 'The Historical Development of Gestalt Psychology' at the Institut d'Histoire des Sciences in Paris in 1933-1934. Merleau-Ponty probably attended those lectures, as his assistance in preparing them for publication was acknowledged. (See Gurwitsch, *op.cit.*, p. 3, n. 1. See also Theodore F. Geraets, *Vers une nouvelle philosophie transcendantale* (The Hague: Martinus Nijhoff, 1971), p. 13).

[5]*Visible*, p. 204 (Working note dated September, 1959).

[6]Merleau-Ponty, *The Primacy of Perception* (Evanston, Ill.: Northwestern University Press, 1964), 'The Child's Relations with Others,' pp. 96-155. (These lectures, as well as 'Phenomenology and the Sciences of Man' in the same volume, are attributed to the year 1960. I take this opportunity to correct the date. Both series of lectures were courses given by Merleau-Ponty at the Sorbonne in 1950-1951).

[7]*Visible*, p. 22.

[8]See Merleau-Ponty's comment in *Visible*, p. 183 (working note dt. February 1959).

[9]*Visible*, p. 165 (working note dt. January 1959).

Study project on the nature of perception*

MAURICE MERLEAU-PONTY

It has seemed to me that in the present state of neurology, experimental psychology (particularly, psychopathology) and philosophy, it would be useful to take up again the problem of perception, and particularly, perception of one's own body.

A doctrine inspired by Critical philosophy treats perception as an intellectual operation through which non-extended data ("sensations") are related and explained in such fashion as to finally constitute an objective universe. So regarded, perception is like an incomplete science, a mediating operation.

Now, experimental investigations carried out in Germany by the "Gestalt" theorists seem to show on the contrary that perception is not an intellectual operation. The "form," on this view, would be present in sense-knowledge itself, and the incoherent "sensations" of traditional psychology would be a gratuitous hypothesis.

The development of neurology has on the other hand clarified the role of the nervous system, whose function seems more and more to be "conduction" of the neural input, and not the function of "elaboration of thinking." While relieving neurologists of the task of looking

*Translation copyright 1980 Forrest W. Williams. From pp. 9-10, Theodore F. Geraets, *Vers une nouvelle philosophie transcendantale*, 1971. With permission of Martinus Nijhoff Publishers, The Hague, copyright 1971; all rights reserved.

for decals of mental functions in localised anatomical functions, and in this sense freeing psychology from "parallelism," this conception brings out the role of "nascent movements," which the nervous system functions to provoke, and which have to accompany every perception. Perception is thus set into a motor framework. The correlation between visual data and those of touch or of muscular feel, which is established, according to the viewpoint prompted by Critical thought, by intellectual activity, memory, and judgment, seems on the contrary to be ensured here by the very functioning of the nervous system. And here, too, the psychologist should perhaps give up his image of a universe of non-extended sensations which "the education of the senses" would convert into a voluminous space by the progressive association of visual data with tactile data.

One would especially have to study the recent literature on the "perception of one's own body." If it seems difficult in a general way to distinguish a matter and a form in sense knowledge, it appears even more difficult regarding perception of one's own body, where extendedness seems obviously to cohere with the sensation.

These observations, and others like them, if a thorough study of the documentation confirms them, would mean going back on the classical postulates of perception. Indeed, the realist philosophers of England and America often insist on what is irreducible to intellectual relations in the sensory and the concrete. The universe of perception could not be assimilated to the universe of science.

In summary, in the present state of philosophy there are grounds for attempting a synthesis of the results of experimental psychology and neurology with respect to the problem of perception, to determine through reflection its precise meaning, and perhaps to recast certain psychological and philosophical notions currently in use.

The nature of perception*

Maurice Merleau-Ponty

A new study of perception seems justified by contemporary developments in philosophical and experimental research:

> —by the appearance, notably in Germany, of new philosophies which call into question the guiding ideas of critical thought, until then dominant in psychology as well as philosophy of perception;
> —by developments in physiology of the nervous system;
> —by developments in mental pathology and child psychology;
> —finally, by progress in a new psychology of perception in Germany (*Gestaltpsychologie*).

During my research this year, such an attempt seemed to me all the more justified because, since the analyses of Lachelier (*L'Observation de Platner*) and Lagneau (*Célèbres Leçons: Cours sur la Perception*) which underlie the theory of perception in Alain, works published in French (for example, the two theses by Duret entitled *Les Facteurs Pratiques de la Croyance dans la Perception* and *L'Objet de la Perception*, Alcan, 1929) take almost no account of recent German work.

*Translation copyright 1980 Forrest W. Williams. From pp. 188-199, Theodore F. Geraets, *Vers une nouvelle philosophie transcendantale*, 1971. With permission of Martinus Nijhoff Pubishers, The Hague, copyright 1971; all rights reserved.

I. PHYSIOLOGY AND PATHOLOGY OF PERCEPTION

Nevertheless, it has not seemed possible to broach this study of perception by way of the physiology of the nervous system nor by way of mental pathology. It seemed to me that both ought to allow us to specify the relation between sense-knowledge and intelligence, by specifying the connection between "projection" and "association." Though the views of C. von Monakow (summarised in Monakow and Mourgue, *Introduction Biologique à l'Etude de la Neurologie et de la Psychopathologie*) and the notion of "chronogenic localisation" furnish guiding concepts for experimentation, they do not yet seem to have yielded specific investigations capable of throwing light on the psychology of perception through brain physiology. It is significant that the overview of H. Piéron (*Le Cerveau et la Pensée*), so precise with regard to "projection," can make only hypothetical points regarding associative phenomena and their relation to the zones of projection.

As for pathology, at least in France, it too cannot provide a guiding thread. The thesis by P. Quercy (*Etudes sur l'Hallucination, v. II: La Clinique*, Alcan, 1930) finally leaves unanswered the question—essential for us—of whether hallucination is a seeing without an object or merely an "attitude" favored by a degradation of beliefs. We can therefore find in it nothing presumptively favorable to a psychology which would make of normal perception a brute given, or, on the contrary, a construction involving the totality of mental activity. Nor can the thesis of H. Wallon (*Stades et Troubles du Développement Psychomoteur et Mental chez l'Enfant*, 1925—since published under the title, *L'Enfant Turbulent*) furnish, in other ways, a decisive orientation. The author reconstitutes the normal development from the subjective to the objective by the method of pathology. But the genesis of external perception remains hidden: it is not yet present, it seems, in the "sensori-motor stage"; in the "projective stage" which follows immediately, it seems fully constituted. For this projective stage is known to us only by analogy to certain epileptic states of mind; now, to be sure, the world of the epileptic child may well be marked by instability and incoherence, caught up as it were in a tyrannical activity—yet it is a world, or rather a mass of external things, and we have not been privy to the genesis of this externality.

Nevertheless, neural physiology and pathology should be able to provide some very important information on two points. On the one hand, there are "localised reflexes" (Piéron), and on the other hand, astereognosias and more generally agnosias. But even in those cases where the nature of the injuries particularly favor the localisation of lesions (bullet wounds or small shell explosions, Gelb and Goldstein, *Psychologische Analysen hirnpathologischer Fälle*, v. I, ch. 1), we should notice that the conjectures always move from the observable sensory or psychic disturbances to merely presumed localisations. Gelb and Goldstein thereby conclude that the first task, before any attempt at physiological interpretation, is to give as exact a description as possible of the disturbed behavior. But the experiments to be undertaken in order to analyse the consciousness of the patient will obviously be suggested by the guiding ideas of a psychology of normal perception (for Gelb and Goldstein, by those of *Gestaltpsychologie*). We are thus brought back to the psychology of the normal—provided always that its conceptions remain subject to the strict control of the facts of pathology.

II. PHILOSOPHY OF PERCEPTION

Psychology of perception is loaded with philosophical presuppositions, which enter in through the seemingly most innocent notions—sensation, mental image, recollection, understood as permanent beings . . . Even apart from any intention of looking into the furthest problems of perception into the meaning of truth in sense knowledge—the psychological problem could not be completely elucidated without resorting to the philosophy of perception. A part of our work this year has therefore been devoted to it.

The phenomenology of Husserl is doubly interesting to us. First, taken in the strict sense assigned to it by Husserl, phenomenology (transcendental phenomenology or "constitutive" phenomenology) is a new philosophy. Its primary problem is not the problem of knowledge, but it gives rise to a theory of knowledge absolutely distinct from that of Critical thought. (E. Fink, "Die phänomenologische Philosophie Husserls in der gegenwärtigen Kritik," in *Kantstudien*, 1933.)† Second, it is said that Husserl is indifferent to psychology. The truth is that he maintains his earlier criticism of "psychologism" and continues to insist on the "reduction" whereby one passes from the natural attitude, which is that of psychology as of all the positive sciences, to the transcendental attitude, which is that of phenomenological philosophy. This difference in attitude suffices to establish a very definite line between phenomenological analyses of perception, for example, and psychological analyses dealing with the same theme.

But, in addition to the fact that he himself has provided an example of a properly psychological analysis of perception (*Ideen zu einer reinen Phänomenologie und phänomenologische Philosophie*, sec. II), Husserl explicitly compares (*ibid*, sec. I, ch. 1) the relations of phenomenology and psychology to those of mathematics and physics, and looks to the development of his philosophy for a renewal of the principles of psychology (cf. *Ideen*, I, II, and the Fink article cited). The properly phenomenological analyses, for example, those of memory and image, which have been published in the *Jahrbuch* (for example, Fink, "Vergegenwärtigung und Bild," *Jahrbuch fur Philosophie und Phänomenologische Forschung*, XI) are not lacking in consequences for psychology.

But one must insist on the fact that in no way do they aim to *replace* psychology. The renewal in question is not an invasion. It is a matter of renewing psychology *on its own terrain*, of bringing to life *the methods proper to it* by analyses which fix the persistently uncertain meaning of fundamental essences such as "representation," "memory," etc. (Linke, "Phänomenologie und Experiment in der Frage der Bewegungsauffassung," *Jahrbuch*, v. II. And by the same author: *Grundfragen der Warhnehmungslehre*, Munich, 1918.) Phenomenology definitely distinguishes "eidetic" method and "inductive" method (that is, experimental method), and never challenges the legitimacy of the latter.

We should not be surprised that the phenomenological movement has even inspired experimental research (for example, Linke, "Die stroboskopische Täuschungen und das Problem des Sehens von Bewegungen," *Psychologische Studien*, v. III, p. 499). It has been maintained (Gurwitsch, "Phänomenologie der Thematik und des Reinen Ich," *Psychologische Forschung*, 1929) that the analyses of Husserl lead to the threshold of *Gestaltpsychologie*. Finally, all "descriptive" psychology is called phenomenology in a very broad sense.

The importance of the phenomenological movement for psychology is scarcely indicated in France by anyone but M. Pradines (*Philosophie de la Sensation*, v. I, especially the "Introduction.") He reproaches the philosophers, from Hume to Bergson, with having too often reduced consciousness to a sum of "impressions" (even in Kant, the "matter" at least of knowledge is something of this sort). As a result, spatiality and in general "signification" are secondary and acquired for consciousness, among the more consistent of these philosophers. Now, for M. Pradines, the appearance of higher senses, essentially different—in the structure of their apparatus—from senses mingled with affect, would be a biological absurdity if from the start it did not pertain to them to be "distance senses," to signify an "object." This philosophy of sensation could be considered a psychological application of the theme of "the intentionality of consciousness" advanced by Husserl.

Phenomenology and the psychology it inspires thus deserve maximum attention in that they can assist us in revising the very notions of consciousness and sensation, in conceiving differently the "cleavage" of consciousness.

III. PSYCHOLOGY OF PERCEPTION

A large part of our work this past year has however been devoted to *Gestaltpsychologie*. The older psychology postulated sensations as primary data of consciousness, supposed to correspond item by item to local excitations of sensory apparatus, such that a given excitation always produced the same sensation (*Konstanzannahme*; cp. Helson, "Studies in the theory of perception; I: The clearness-context theory," *Psychological Review*, January 1932; also Köhler, *Gestalt Psychology*, New York & London, 1929). To get from these alleged "givens" to the scenario of things as we actually perceive them, it was necessary to conjecture an "elaboration" of sensations by memory, by knowledge, by judgment—of "matter" by "form"; a passage from the subjective "mosaic" (Wertheimer) to the world of objects. The school with which we are concerned explains for one thing, by the psychological factor called "Gestalt," what the older psychology referred to interpretation and judgment. The "Gestalt" is a spontaneous organisation of the sensory field which has supposed "elements" dependent on "wholes" which are themselves articulated within more extensive wholes. This organisation is not like a form imposing itself upon a heterogeneous matter; there is no matter without form; there are only organisations, more or less stable, more or less articulated. But these definitions only sum up abstractly experimental investigations which can be followed up in two main directions:

1. *Object.*

Our everyday perception is not of a mosaic of qualities but of an ensemble of distinct objects. What makes one part of the field thus set off and differentiated, according to traditional psychology, is the memory of prior experiences, knowledge. For *Gestaltpsychologie* an object does not stand out because of its "signification" ("meaning"), but because it possesses in our perception a special structure: the structure of "figure-ground." One determines the objective conditions—independent of will and intellect—which are necessary and sufficient to engender the "figure" structure (for example, the maximum and optimal distance at which several points are *seen* as a figure, a constellation—Wertheimer). This very structure is analysed, is definable by certain *sensible* properties: for example, the differential threshold is higher for the background colors than for the figure colors. According to Gelb and Goldstein, *certain* psychic blindnesses, which had been interpreted as an inability to "project" the appropriate memories on the sensation, would be instead a perturbation of the structural processes just noted. (W. Köhler, *Gestalt Psychology*, London & New York, 1929. "An Aspect of Gestalt Psychology," by C. Murchison, in *Psychologies of 1925*. K. Gottschaldt, "Ueber den Einfluss der Erfahrung auf die Wahrnehmung von Figuren," *Psych. Forschung*, VIII, 1927. Sander, "Experimentelle Ergebnisse der Gestaltpsychologie," in *Bericht ueber den X Kongress f*ür experimentelle Psychologie, 1927. Gelb & Goldstein, *op. cit.*)

This "figure-ground" structure is itself only a particular case of the spontaneous organisation of sensory fields. In general, it must be said that primitive perception bears rather on relations than on isolated terms—*visible*, not *conceived* relations. (Köhler, "Optischer Untersuchungen am Schimpansen und am Haushuhn," 1915; "Nachweis einfacher Strukturfunktionen beim Schimpansen und beim Haushuhn," 1918.) These conceptions render Weber's Law more understandable and, by the same token, are thereby confirmed: the discontinuity of the conscious changes corresponding to a continuous variation in the stimulus is explainable by certain structural laws (the law of levelling, the law of accentuation), and finally appears as a particular case of the general law of "pregnancy" established by Wertheimer. (Koffka, "Perception: An Introduction to Gestalt Theory," Psychological Bulletin, XIX, 1922. Sander, *op. cit.*)

2. *Space and movement.*

The perception of space is a prime site of intellectualist elaborations. The distance of an object, for example, is referred back to an instantaneous judgment which is based on signs, such as apparent size or a disparity of retinal images, and which concludes how many steps we would have to take to touch the object. Space is no longer an object of vision but an object of thought. Now, a penetrating critique of "disparity of images" (Koffka, "Some Problems of Space Perception," in *Psychologies of 1930*) leads to the admission that the disparity of images, even if it is a condition of depth perception, is not the occasion of a judgment, but the cause of a neural process of which we know only the conscious outcome, in the form of an impression of depth. In reality, the phenomenon of depth perception has a structure analogous to those just noted. This is particularly well demonstrated where an object is seen through a nearer transparent object: the seeing of depth can be produced or cancelled by modifying the color of the surrounding field. (Cf. Koffka, *ibid*; Tudor-Hart, "Studies in transparency, form, and colours," *Psychologische Forschung*, 1928.) Here, once again, Gestalt psychology is in a position to interpret important findings previously made: those of Schumann and his school which disclosed a sort of space-quality in perception. (Schumann, Fuchs, Katz, Jaensch, de Karpinska, *et al* in *Zeitschrift für Psychologie und Physiologie der Sinnesorganen*.) Although this research may have had some influence on the work of Lavelle (*La Perception Visuelle de la Profondeur*, Strasbourg, 1921), and although Pradines has supplied a bibliography, they themselves remain unknown in France, and the thesis of Mlle. R. Déjean (*Etude Psychologique de la Distance dans la Vision*, Paris, 1926) does not deal with them, even though she also tends to posit distance as inherent in seeing.

Supposing that we always judged what we saw by what was painted upon the retina, and that points stretching into depth were projected onto a single plane, one indeed had to suppose that the subject reconstituted the depth, got to it by means of a conclusion, but did not see it. By contrast, and for the very same reason, the immediate perception of width and height presented no difficulty. But we no longer have any reason to consider depth to be derived and ulterior. Perhaps it should even be seen as a more simple mode of perception than perceiving surfaces. Gelb and Goldstein (op. cit., I, pp. 334-419, "Uber den Wegfall der Wahrnehmung von Oberflächenfarben") show that seeing surface colors is a relatively fragile organisation, easily altered in certain pathological cases, when it gives way to a seeing of "thick" colors [*épaisses*]—all the "thicker" as they are less pale [*clair*]. (On the relations of paleness—or more exactly, of *Eindringlichkeit*—and apparent "thickness" [*épaisseur*], see Ackermann, *Psychologische Forschung*, 1924, and Tudor-Hart, *loc. cit.*)

Moreover, direct study of our perception of space in terms of height and width had already uncovered structural phenomena. The characteristics of "vertical," "horizontal," or "oblique" are conferred upon the lines of the visual field, declared the earlier psychology, by a mental reference to the meridian of our retina, to the axis of our head and our body. For Wertheimer, on the contrary, certain important points of our sensory field ("anchor" points) determine a sort of "spatial level" and the lines of the field immediately feature the indices "upward," "downward," without judgments or comparisons. ("Experimentelle Studien über das Sehen von Bewegung; Anhang," in *Zeitschrift für Psychologie*, 1912.) Experimentation shows disruptions of this equilibrium or changes of this level, and shows that in such cases there is no question of an intellectual operation, of a change in a system of coordinates.

Similarly, in a series of methodical experiments the same author disclosed, in so-called "stroboscopic" movement, a "pure movement," a movement without a moved. Our perception of movement could not therefore be assimilated to an estimate of increasing distance between two points which alone are perceived, that is, to movement as defined by the physicist. It should be stressed that in this analysis, as in the preceding ones, the whole concern of the Gestalt psychologists is in experiences which their principles render possible and which are not otherwise accounted for. Nothing could be less like a hasty appeal to something *"sui generis."* (Wetheimer, *loc.cit.*)

These remarks do not claim to exhaust the analysis of perceptual space according to Gestalt psychology. We have mainly drawn on new findings which fall under traditional considerations. But it has also opened new chapters, for example, that of the statics inherent in our perception (Köhler, *L'Intelligence des Singes Supérieurs*).

3. *Gestalt psychology and child psychology.*

The idea of a "syncretic perception" in children (Claparède, 1908), confirmed by more recent research, and in particular by a study of stroboscopic movement in relation to children (Meidi & Tobler, *Archives de Psychologie*, 1931-32) collided with research which indicated on the contrary a highly sensitive perception of details among children. The notion of Gestalt seems capable of doing justice to both lines of investigation. For syncretic perception (of an uniform bloc) and analytical perception (where only juxtaposed details exist), rather than conflicting, as often supposed, together contrast with the structured perception of the adult in which the ensembles are articulated and the details are organised.

The child's perception is nonetheless already organised, but in its own fashion. And a principle offered by Gestalt psychology to psychogenetic theory is that development does not occur by simple attachment or addition, but by reorganisation. (Koffka, *Die Grundlagen der psychischen Entwicklung*, 1921; *Journal de Psychologie*, 1924.) For perception, a world of connected objects would not appear out of a mosaic of impressions, but better articulated ensembles would appear out of poorly or otherwise related ensembles. One could thus join up with certain observations by Piaget (*La Représentation du Monde chez l'Enfant*) which Piaget's own formulations do not always express accurately. If one says, for example, that the child's perception of the world is "egocentric," this is true enough, in the sense that the world of the child ignores the simplest criteria of objectivity of the adult. But precisely to be unacquainted with adult objectivity is not to live in oneself, it is to practice an unmeasured objectivity; the notion of egocentricity should not be allowed to suggest the old idea of a consciousness enclosed in "its states." Observations by P. Guillaume (*Journal de Psychologie*, 1924) point on the contrary to the precociousness of behavior adapted to space. It is significant that H. Wallon, who seemed to conceive the genesis of objective perception along traditional lines, as a passage from the internal to the external (Wallon, "De l'image au réel chez l'enfant," *Revue de Philosophie*) implicitly restricts this thesis in his latest work, *Les Origines de Caractère chez l'Enfant*. He sees the child—from the age of three or four months, it seems, that is, "when there begins the myelin joining of the interoceptive and proprioceptive domains, on the one hand, and the exteroceptive domain on the other" (p. 176)—"turned toward a source of excitations, toward a motif in motion, and bent on experiencing its various possibilities" (p. 180).

4. *Gestalt psychology and theory of knowledge.*

This wholly new conception of the content of consciousness has important consequences in theory of sense knowledge. These consequences have not yet been clearly shown. Within Gestalt psychology the issue is hardly discussed. The usual attitude of psychologists is adopted: the distinction between a world of things and an immanent consciousness. The organisation or structuring of consciousness is explained by central physiological phenomena (Wertheimer's "transverse" phenomena, cp. *loc. cit.*), whose existence is, moreover, much contested. Those outside Gestalt psychology have maintained that its problem of knowledge is couched in the same terms as Kant (Gutwitsch, *op. cit.*). We must look, we believe, in a different direction, for a very different solution.

†[Note added in margin of written text:]
   Cf. Lévinas, *La Théorie de l'intuition dans la phénoménologie de Husserl.* G. Gurvitsch, "La Phénoménologie de Husserl," *Revue de Métaphysique,* 1928. J. Héring, *Phénoménologie et Philosophie religieuse,* and Husserl, *Méditations Cartésiennes.*

Books and articles [in the order cited]:

Lachelier, Jules. *L'Observation de Platner,* in *Oeuvres,* II, 65-104 (Paris: Alcan, 1933).

Lagneau, Jules. *Célèbres Leçons: Cours sur la Perception* (Nîmes, 1926.

Duret, *Les facteurs pratiques de la crovance dans la perception (Paris: Alcan, 1929).*

Monakow, Mourgue. *Introduction biologique à l'étude de la neurologie et de la psychopathologie* (Paris: Alcan, 1928).

Piéron, H. *Le cerveau et la pensée* (Paris: Alcan, 1923; 2nd ed.).

Quercy, P. *L'haullucination; II: La clinique* (Paris: Alcan, 1930).

Wallon, H. *L'enfant turbulent* (Paris: Alcan, 1925).

Gelb & Goldstein. *Psychologische Analysen hirnpathologischer Fälle,* Leipzig, 1920.

Fink, E. "Die phänomenologische philosophie Edmund Husserls in der gegenwärtigen Kritik," in *Kantstudien* (XXXVIII, 1933), 319-383.

Husserl, E. Ideen zu einer reinen Phänomenologie und phänomenologische Philosophie (*Jahrbuch für Philosophie und Phämenologische Forschung,* I, 1913, 1-323).

Fink, E. "Vergegenwärtigung und Bild," in *J. für Phil. u. phän. Forsch.,* II (1930), 239-309.

Linke, "Die stroboskopische Täuschungen und das Problem des Sehens von Bewegungen," in *Psychologische Studien* (Leipzig: Engelmann, 1907), II.

Gurwitsch, A. "Phänomenologie der Thematik und des Reinen Ich. Studien uber Beziehungen von Gestalttheorie und Phänomenologie," in *Psychologische Forschung,* 1929, 279-381.

Pradines, M. *Philosophie de la sensation* (Paris: Les Belles Lettres, 1928-1932).

Helson, "Studies in the Theory of Perception. I: The Clearness-context Theory," in Psychological Review (1932), 44-72.

Köhler, W. *Gestaltpsychologie* [*Gestalt Psychology*] (New York & London, 1929).

Köhler, W. "An aspect of Gestalt Psychology," in C. Murchison (ed., Psychologies of 1930 (London: 1930), 163-195.

Köhler, W. "Some Tasks of Gestalt Psychology," in *ibid,* 143-160.

Gottschaldt, K. "Über den Einfluss der Erfahrung auf die Wahrnehmung von Figuren," in *Psychologische Forschung* (VIII, 1927), 261-317.

Sander, F. *Experimentelle Ergebnisse der Gestaltpsychologie* (Jena: Fischer, 1928).

Köhler, W. "Optische Untersuchungen am Schimpansen und am Haushuhn," in *Abhandlungen der Königlichen preussischen Akademie der Wissenschaften*, 1916.

Köhler, W. "Nachweis einfacher Strukturfunktionen beim Schimpansen und beim Haushuhn," in *ibid*, 1918.

Koffka, K. "Perception: An Introduction to Gestalt Theory," in *Psychological Bulletin* (XIX, 1922), 531-585.

Koffka, K. "Some Problems of Space Perception," in C. Murchison, *op. cit.*, 161-187.

Tudor-Hart, B. "Studies in Transparency, Form and Colour," in *Psychologische Forschung*, 1928, 255-298.

Lavelle, Louis. *La perception visuelle de la profondeur* (Strasbourg, 1921).

Déjean, R. *Etude psychologique de la distance dans la vision* (Paris, 1926).

Ackermann, "Farbschwelle und Feldstruktur" in *Psychologische Forschung*, 1924, 44-84.

Wertheimer, M. "Experimentelle Studien über das Sehen von Bewegung," in *Zeitschrift für Psychologie* (LXI, 1912), 161-265; "Anhang," 253-265.

Köhler, W. *L'intelligence des singes supérieurs* (Paris: Alcan, 1927; tr. P. Guillaume).

Meili & Tobler. "Les mouvements stroboscopiques chez les enfant," in *Archives de Psychologie* (XXIII, 1931-1932), 131-156.

Meili. "Les perceptions des enfants et la psychologie de la Gestalt," in *ibid*, 25-44.

Koffka, K. *Die Grundlagen der psychischen Entwicklung* (Osterwick am Harz, 1921).

Koffka, K. "Théorie de la Forme et psychologie de l'enfant," in *Journal de psychologie normale et pathologique* (XXI, 1924).

Piaget, J. *La représentation du monde chez l'enfant* (Paris: Alcan, 1926).

Guillaume, P. "Le problème de la perception de l'espace et la psychologie de l'enfant," in *Jour. de psych. norm. et path.* (XXI, 1924), 112-134.

Wallon, H. "De l'image au réel chez l'enfant," in *Revue de Philosophie* (?).

Wallon, H. *Les origines du caractère chez l'enfant* (Paris: Boivin, 1934).

Perception and Structure in Merleau-Ponty

BERNHARD WALDENFELS
Ruhr-Universität Bochum

More decisively than many others, Merleau-Ponty pursued phenomenology throughout his life; more decisively than many others, however, he worked on an internal transformation of phenomenology up to his sudden death. This attempt finally led him to the *limits of phenomenology*, to the point at which non-phenomenology asserts itself within phenomenology itself. As he notes in his late essay about Husserl, "The philosopher bears his shadow, which is not simply the merely factual absence of future light" (SG 225/178). The shadowing-forth of the phenomena turns into a deeper shadow; the things themselves cast their shadows.

Merleau-Ponty's attempt to open up an approach to the phenomena can be characterized as a search for a third dimension this side of subject and object. In 1952 he wrote:

> Thus, on the one hand it is necessary to follow the spontaneous development of the positive sciences by asking whether man is really reduced to the status of an object here, and on the other hand we must reconsider the reflexive and philosophical attitude by investigating whether it really gives us the right to define ourselves as unconditioned and timeless subjects. It is possible that these converging investigations will finally lead us to see a milieu which is common to philosophy and the positive sciences, and that something like a third dimension opens up, this side of the pure subject and the pure object, where our activity and our passivity, our autonomy and our dependence no longer contradict one another (Titres et travaux, P. 5).[1]

This motif is to provide the guiding thread for the following reflections. I have a twofold goal. In the *first* place, I shall try to show how the attempt to conceive of the phenomenality of the phenomena in terms of structure and form (Gestalt) brings with it a radicalizing of phenomenology. Here we encounter a series of questions concerning the status of phenomenology, questions which may determine the survival chances of phenomenology. In the *second* place, I shall try to use these concepts to decipher Merleau-Ponty's thought in a way that provides us with a focal point in terms of which a series of beginnings and individual attempts can find their proper place in a theoretical field. Here we shall encounter a special difficulty. Merleau-Ponty's work, especially the early work, resembles in many respects a palimpsest in which various strata are superimposed on one another. There simply is no straight and clear-cut development, to say nothing of a closed system which stands there once and for all.

I would like to develop these themes in three stages. In the first part, I shall deal with the *structures of behaviour* as they appear in Merleau-Ponty's earliest work; here we shall have to pay special attention to the degree to which later developments are already anticipated. In the second part I shall deal with the *forms and structures of perception*; in this thematic, which is characteristic for the *Phénoménologie de la perception*, we find an unusual amount of reciprocal overlapping of old and new motifs, which leads to ambiguities and a certain indecisiveness. The third part deals, under the title *structures of being*, with the new beginning which is to be found in *Le visible et l'invisible*, where Merleau-Ponty expressly distances himself from the earlier remnants of a philosophy of consciousness. In this late work, which exists only in fragments, much remains on the level of sketches, such that interpretation is almost identical with a further development of the thoughts.

I. STRUCTURES OF BEHAVIOR

The early work, *La structure du comportement*, which was completed in 1938, is centered on the concept of behavior: the behavior of an organism toward its environment, that of a human being to his world. In characterizing behavior, the concepts *structure* and *form*, as well as the concepts of meaning or sense, play a decisive role, not merely as an aid to description within the framework of an already existing theory, but rather as a means of articulating a new kind of theoretical field. This field can be characterized as a third dimension which lies on this side of the split into pure nature and pure consciousness, pure externality and pure internality.

Under the influence of A. Gurwitsch, and in much the same way, Merleau-Ponty takes up new lines of thought within the empirical sciences: Gestalt theory, above all that of the Berlin School, the research into environments by the group around Buytendijk, the Gestaltkreis theory of V. v. Weizsäcker, the structural psychopathology of K. Goldstein and his school. A penetrating interpretation of these lines of research demonstrates that the naturalism of pure facts disappears, but without leading to an appeal to an intellectualism of pure forms of consciousness. It is of decisive significance that, from the very beginning, Merleau-Ponty looked for and found a mode of access to phenomenology via the empirical field of the behavioral sciences. In this respect he proved to be less defensive than Husserl, who never really took note of these new developments.[2]

We shall see how the ground of a pure philosophy of consciousness is left behind in this way, and how the concept of the phenomenon experiences a corresponding change of accent. I shall begin with some characteristic aspects of the concept of structure or form.

1. *Formal Characteristics*: Structure and form belong to a middle dimension, they are neither 'things', i.e. pure existents, complexions of externally connected data, nor 'ideas', i.e. products of an intellectual synthesis. Rather, they are the result of a process of the self-organization of experiential, actional and linguistic fields, which is not governed by pre-existing principles (SC 53/49) and yet itself is prior to any possible disintegration into disparate elements and individual events. Husserl's goal of a "Logos of the aesthetic world" begins to assume a concrete form here, and the transcendental dimension is thereby shifted into a pre-egological region.

2. *Horizontal Dimension*: Structure and form are not, as Husserl's repeated criticism of Gestalt theory (CM, §§16, 20) suggested, pre-given wholes which repeat atomism on a higher level. Rather, structuring and the formation of the Gestalt themselves concern the organization of world and surrounding world (ex. in the form of stimuli), and they extend physiologically into the anatomical structures of the brain. Finally, they create an internal relation between specific milieu and corresponding behavioral style. Thus, we are here confronted with a *structure of structures* as a horizontal bond between bodily behavior and world.

3. *Vertical Dimension*: The various types of phenomena and behavior refer to various levels of structure; infrastructures are integrated in superstructures, although higher and lower cannot be causally derived from one another. There results a structural composi-

tion as a vertical tissue of specific strata of phenomena and behavior, which itself is based on a structural genesis.

Accordingly, phenomenology appears as a "description of structures" (SC 170/157), structure itself as "fundamental reality" (SC 226/209), where "fundamental" cannot be understood in the traditional sense of fundamental facts or first principles. The decisive condition for the appearance of something is the fact that something stands out against something else. Thus, figure and background embody a *primordial difference*; formlessness, which can only be thought as a limiting experience, would not be a raw chaos, but rather a monotony which would transform seeing into not-seeing. Composition and decomposition of the experiential world takes place as a process of *differentiation* and *dedifferentiation*. It is not primarily a question of whether or not that which is meant is there or not, whether it is given in an originary or derivative manner, whether it itself is present or is represented by something else, as is assumed by a theory of perception which places presence in the center; rather, the decisive thing is the degree of differentiation in experience and the direction this process of differentiation takes. The formation of sense becomes a process of continual *structuring, restructuring* or *transformation*, which at the same time extends to the world and behavior, and brings about an organization and articulation of specific experiential fields. Elementary examples of this would be the development of a system of colors or a system of sounds.

This structural mode of thinking demonstrates its fruitfulness in the various registers of experience, which exhibit corresponding moments on the basis of their homologous structuring. I would like to mention a few concrete applications here; we shall see clearly the manner in which traditional modes of thought begin to break down.

1. *Theory of Meaning*: Meaning is thought in terms of structure, as "incarnate meaning", which—as for example the physiognomy of a circular form or the untying of a knot as a practical task—is not absorbed in an "ideal meaning." On this level, structure is nothing more than the contingent arrangement of a sensuous material (SC 223/206); an autochthonous sense which lives in the behavior itself is embodied in it. The language-analytical mode of analysis finds its limits here, since talk about experiential forms can never imply that they represent an exclusive achievement of language.[3]

2. *Consciousness*: Consciousness is not a pure consciousness *of* structures; it has a structure of its own,—e.g. "cognitive structures," as contemporary psychology says—, *in* which our experience and behavior moves or which it runs up against; thus, consciousness is not

the locus of an embracing survey. Accordingly, reflexion and liberation do not coincide with a mere change of consciousness, an "ideal
liberation"; wherever cognitive and practical structures or modes of
organization change, there is a "real *Umgestaltung*" [transforma-
tion—the original uses the German term] at work, and only in this way
can it come to a "real liberation" (SC 238/221). Goldstein's research
into pathology, which takes possible restrictions and removal of
restrictions in the behavioral milieu as their point of departure,
parallel insights of Marx here, in as much as Marx shifts consciousness
into the real processes of life, from which it can only apparently be
separated. A pure self-transparency and self command would be
nothing more than a "lucid dream" (SC 240/223) whose realization
shatters on the fact that we have to deal with acquired and resistence
structures which we cannot put behind us or put out of play, but at
most transform.

3) *Encounter with the Other:* Since the structures of behavior can be
read off of behavior itself, the alternative of introspection and external observation proves to be false; in this way the primacy of self-
experience as a primal presence which expands itself secondarily to an
appresentation of the Other is shaken (SC 197f., 239/182f., 221-2).

4. *Symbolism of Behavior:* The distinction between signal and sym-
bol refers to various levels of behavior in which the subject more or
less detaches himself from the situation (SC 130ff./120ff.). Mere
gradations of consciousness, which one might accept following Leib-
niz, are not sufficient to explain these different structural
achievements, and a rigid concept of reason, which creates a chasm
between animal and human behavior would be totally inappropriate.[4]

5) *Pathology of Behavior:* Leaning heavily on the work of K. Goldstein, Merleau-Ponty takes up the general point that in the case of
pathological disturbances, it is not a matter of a mere breakdown of
functions, but rather of structural disturbances which lead to an im-
poverishment of structures (loss of differentiation), to an emancipa-
tion of partial structures (dissociation), to the development of replacement structures, and so on. Behavior carries out specific achievements
here too, and does not simply gradually fade away into the amor-
phous. Finally, a structural mode of considering the phenomena
allows us to take account of the ambivalent character of disease.
Anomalies are thus not to be interpreted as mere changes in an existing normality, but also as possible transitions to new normalities
(cf. Blankenburg).

But in the end we must ask whether Merleau-Ponty has drawn the
necessary consequences from this structural line of thought. In this

context I am thinking especially of the two-fold function which is ascribed to consciousness. In the first place, on the descriptive level, consciousness appears as a structure among structures, and phenomenology accordingly claims to be a description of structures. The structural order assumes here the position of a transcendental and constituting subjectivity (cf. Levinas in the Forward to Geraets, p. XI). But on the other hand, in the course of a transcendental turn consciousness expands to become a *universal milieu*, and phenomenology assumes the role of an "inventory of consciousness" (SC 215/199). We must add, however, that according to its most fundamental form consciousness is perceptual consciousness. But why this holding fast to consciousness as the fundamental fact? Because the insistence on an outside of consciousness cannot initially be thought of as other than a fall back into objectivism or naturalism. Other modes of thought appear first at a later stage, where the recourse to symbolic frameworks for interpretation and institutionalized rule systems allow consciousness to be decentrized in a different manner, namely in terms of "another scene" which no longer presents us with a merely natural externality. Here, on this early level of reflection, the third dimension which Merleau-Ponty is searching for is won by means of a mere weakening of the principle of consciousness; the known is outweighed by the experienced, the intellectual by structure; this is certainly not a radical revision. With perceptual consciousness we have reached the point at which the *Phenomenology of Perception* begins with a greater one-sidedness.

II. GESTALT AND STRUCTURE OF PERCEPTION

In the *Phenomenology of Perception*, Merleau-Ponty no longer begins with a description of world and behavioral structures from an external point of view. Rather, he goes directly to perception itself and unfolds the relation to the world from the point of view of experience itself (cf. "Un inédit..." 403/5). The third dimension, which discloses itself from the standpoint of experience, is straightforwardly characterized as incarnate consciousness, which corresponds to an *incarnate sense*. This gives rise to a position which is not inappropriately called "phénoménologie existentielle". "Existence" here refers to a "third term" between the in-itself and the for-itself (PP 142/122). What Merleau-Ponty undertakes from this point of view is well known, and need not be repeated here. At this point I would merely like to show how in the *Phenomenology of Perception*, the richest and most detailed, but also probably the most ambiguous of Merleau-

Ponty's works, a two-fold tendency is at work: a compromising tendency, which is burdenend by older ideas, and a radical, progressive tendency, whose effect on Merleau-Ponty's general conception of phenomenology calls for careful scrutiny.[5]

1) *Compromising Tendency*: The standpoint of consciousness is weakened by shifting the locus of the formation of sense into an anterior domain (Vorbereich), which is to be understood synchronically as a founding stratum, diachronically as pre-history. A meaningfully structured world is always already pregiven, because and insofar as I and the other are pregiven to ourselves and to one another, pregiven as bodily existence, which takes on a prepersonal, prereflexive character. The process of forming sense has thus always already begun, although only sketchily and characterized by an open ambiguity; every positing of sense is thus a continuation, a "re-prise," not a pure positing. With this internal reference of the telos to an arché which eludes our grasp, every absolute transparency is excluded (cf. Waldenfels 1968).

This optics is expressed in a variety of motifs. Perception is a "primal text"; structure is irreducible and continues to be differentiated from intellectual meaning; functioning intentionality precedes act-intentionality; a "silent cogito" constitutes the background of all speaking; an anonymous co-existence and an "in-between" (intermonde) is the foundation for the distinction ego—alter ego, etc. This lies squarely along Husserl's line of thought, which more and more shifts the locus of originary sense formation to a pre-predicative level, and which gives the lifeworld as well as the original belief in the world an increasing weight (PP 61f., 419/49f., 365). Accordingly, the *phenomenological reduction* signifies a break with the world which makes the prior connection to the world visible and teaches us the decisive lesson that the reduction itself cannot be completely carried through. (Later he will write: "the incompleteness of the reduction ...is the reduction itself, the rediscovery of vertical being" (VI 232/178). The *eidetic reduction* is not an independent goal, but is rather the means with which the facticity of the world can be grasped. Thus, there is no reason to give up the transcendental viewpoint on the basis of these considerations, for the tension between active sense-giving and passive pre-givenness can be carried out within the life of transcendental sense formation. This is an echo of Husserl's return from the I to a pre-ego and an anonymous life.

Now why is this merely a compromise? Because the weakening of the point of view of consciousness continues the philosophy of consciousness and works against it at the same time. The tendency of the philosophy of consciousness continues in the concern for presence and self-presence, in which consciousness is characterized precisely as "présence de moi á moi" (PP X/XV),[6] for every pre-givenness is referred to an I which takes up the pre-given. The prefix "pre-" continues to refer to a consciousness; it is, as Freud would say, merely a "pre-consciousness." The laws governing the structuring of consciousness are delegated to the body in a watered-down form, but consciousness retains its central position. The phenomenological reduction cannot be completely carried out, but the attempt is not abandoned. Thus, every "pre-" can be incorporated into the life of consciousness as its underground and prehistory. Temporality, which bridges the hiatus between immanence and transcendence, becomes the solution to all riddles (cf. PP 417f./363f.). To be sure, we are faced with a philosophy of *concrete* subjectivity, but it is still a philosophy of subjectivity. Within the third dimension, which was to undercut the opposition of subject and object, there remains a priority of one pole.

And at this point certain difficulties appear which have a thoroughly symptomatic character. Clinging to a goal which must remain elusive, since the beginning is not available to personal initiative, leads to a kind of *unhappy consciousness* (VI 232/178), to a "utopia of possession at a distance" (EP 79/58). Accordingly, the so-called middle term is subjected to *fluctuating determinations*. The third dimension is specified in terms of the extremes by means of the method of the neither-nor (neither nature nor spirit, etc.), but there is no sign that it might be possible to conceive of this region radically in its own terms. Thus, we find circular determinations, which aim at an exchange between body and world, but remain caught in a kind of "double view": " We choose our world and the world chooses us" (PP 518/454), or: "The sensible gives back to me what I lent it, but this is only what I took from it in the first place" (PP 248/214). The symbiotic connection between I and world which is intended here can be articulated only with great difficulty. Finally, we come upon residues which are very difficult to integrate. We hear of an "underground of non-human nature", in which human beings are rooted; and again, this nature is interpreted as "pre-world" (pré-monde, PP. 372f./322f.). The objective body appears in opposition to the phenomenal body as a mere "impoverished structure" (PP 403/351); but this is most certainly not enough, since there is also an encounter with the materiality of the body (cf. the critique in Plügge, p. 34ff.). Merleau-Ponty himself later spoke of a "bad ambiguity", which arises from the fact that perception is thought as a "mixture of finitude and universality, of internality and externality" ("Un inedit..." 409/11). "Mixture"—that recalls Descartes, who tried to deal with the initial dualism of mind and body in this way. Though this charge cannot be made against the concrete analyses of the *Phenomenology of Perception*, it does indicate a theoretical insufficiency which cannot be dealt with in a purely descriptive manner, since certain patterns of thought are reflected in the interpretation of that which is described.[7]

This compromising attitude is also reflected in the philosophy of history and in the political reflections and comments.[8] Marxist wait and see attitudes result from holding on to the old (Hegelian) ideas, to the possibility of a solution to the riddle of history, although the emphasis on the open ambiguity of all historical situations and the inertia of specific institutions runs counter to this way of seeing things. Merleau-Ponty attempted to deal with certain obsessions in the *Adventures of the Dialectic*, but without being able to do more than hint at alternatives.

2) *Radical Tendency*: It would certainly not be true to simply say that the *Phenomenology of Perception* remained stuck in old assumptions. Merleau-Ponty's theory contains many radical moments which introduce a transformation of the theoretical field. Significantly, these elements are closely connected with the theory of form and structure.

For Merleau-Ponty, phenomenology means that we are no longer dealing with a *pre-existent reason* which precedes the concrete and contingent course of experience. In the Forward to the *Phenomenology of Perception* he writes: "The phenomenological world is not the bringing to explicit expression of a pre-existing being, but the laying down of being. Philosophy is not the reflection of a pre-existing truth, but, like art, the act of bringing truth into being" (PPXV/XX; cf. Taminiaux 1976, 100).[9] Thus, we are referred to that which takes place in experience itself, to a rationality which arises within experience, and there is no model to which we can appeal, no prior region to which we can withdraw. From this point of view, Gestalt and structure gain a fundamental significance. The appearance of the phenomena of structure "is not the external unfolding of a pre-existing reason," and the Gestalt "is the very appearance of the world and not the condition of its possibility; it is the birth of a norm and is not realized according to a norm; it is the identity of the external and the internal and not the projection of the internal in the external" (PP 74/60-1).[10] The concept of immediacy is thus subjected to a clear reinterpretation; that which lies at the beginning of experience is nothing other than "the meaning, the structure, the spontaneous arrangement of parts" (PP 70/58).

If this is the case, and if the Gestalt does not mirror a pre-existent order, but rather establishes an order, and if "showing itself" is identical with "articulating itself," then we find ourselves in an anterior field, "on this side of true and false" ("Un inédit..." 401/3), "on this side of yes and no" (VI 138/02).[11] But can we still speak of perceptual intentions in such a self-evident manner, connecting this with a corresponding perceptual *consciousness*? In Husserl perception signifies: that which we mean is given to us in bodily presence, and thus fulfills our intention. Truth thus means that something presents itself in the same manner as it was meant (truth as adequation). Is a scheme of this kind, which still reckons with a duality of subjectivity and objectivity, still applicable? What does the formation of Gestalt and structure mean other than precisely the organization of an experiential field *within* which the I appears under specific conditions, but without steering this process as a whole? A. Gurwitsch (1975) drew such conclusions. And further: can figures which appear for the first time be true or false? Would this not mean measuring perception against a "non-existent standard?" (cf. Nietzsche, Werke III, 317).

To be sure, in connection with Merleau-Ponty's distinction between "parole parlante" (speaking speech) and "parole parlée" (spoken speech), one can speak of a "perception percevante" (perceiving perception) and a "perception perçue" (perceived perception). There are "true" figures and a corresponding understanding, but only in an already established experiential world, just as there are correct sentences only within an already established linguistic world.[12] Original perception thus remains, in opposition to "empirical or secondary perception", a "creative operation which is co-productive of its own standards" (PP 53f., 74/43, 61),[13]—we might add: just like very originary artistic expression. And here we should not think merely of great cultural upheavals and individual works of genius, but also of the slow erosion and shifts which change our everyday seeing, acting, speaking and feeling. Kant's opposition of transcendental idealism and empirical realism returns here in a transformed and more concrete form. But perception is no longer primarily presentation, i.e. presentification of something which up to then was absent or hidden, but rather *articulation*, a kind of formation of a text. The "original text" of perception (PP 29/21) is thus not already inscribed on the things themselves, but is rather subject to a "perceptual syntax" (PP 45/36).

In addition, one can and must mention that every production of Gestalts, be it more productive or more reproductive, is subject to specific impulsive tendencies, interests and restrictive conditions, such as those that are expressed in the laws governing the Gestalt. But

Gestalt rules are no more fixed goals and norms that simply direct vision than are linguistic rules. Inventive and habitual seeing, speaking and acting are always more than correct seeing, speaking and acting. The question concerning the specific mechanism of sense-formation cannot be answered exclusively with reference to general laws and pregiven levels of sense or material, since it is here a matter of at most necessary, but by no means sufficient conditions. Formation and structuring processes never occur arbitrarily and suspended from their situation, but they are by no means restricted to the application of pregiven rules to pregiven situations, for as long as they do not petrify to stereotypes and formuli, they move in a more or less open space, and it is up to them to "define" the situation in the first place, as A. Schutz says.[14]

All of these considerations confront us with the question whether the third dimension which we are searching for must not be thought in terms of a radical renunciation of a centering consciousness, a renunciation of a "natural I" in the form of bodily existence, which is thought as a preliminary form of consciousness. These questions become pressing in Merleau-Ponty's late work.

III. STRUCTURES OF BEING

The radicalization of the mode of thought and seeing which is initiated in the late work *The Visible and the Invisible* does, to be sure, continue in the same direction as earlier attempts, but certain ambiguities of the older theory of perception are examined more critically. Again, thought in terms of structure plays a special role. An increasing familiarity with the structural linguistics of Saussure and Jakobson, a sympathetic relationship to the ethnological structural analyses of Lévi-Strauss, and a renewed, deeper engagement with Freud are decisive.[15] Of special importance, however, is the fact that the structures are less and less viewed as subjective achievements, but rather are relocated in Being itself. One can speak of a new *ontology*. But just what ontology is here—Merleau-Ponty characterizes it as "indirect ontology" (VI 233/179) or as "intra-ontology" (VI 280/227)—, can only be understood in terms of a deepening of a mode of questioning which undercuts the opposition of subject and object. The decisive turn consists in the fact that the third dimension is no longer searched for in an anterior domain, which would always remain something like an advance guard of consciousness, but in an *in between*. The emphasis on topological as opposed to purely chronological points of view is an index for this turn, which has a series of implications.

1) *Meaning, sense, essence and concept* are now thought strictly in terms of Gestalt, as *deviations* and *differences* within a field. This comes to expression in numerous phrases and formulations. Meanings are "écarts définis" (VI 291/238), essence appears as "écart des paroles" (VI 157/117), the meaning as "structure formulée" (VI 192/237). There is no positivity, no intuitiveness of these structures, but only "structures du vide" (VI 289/235); the "hinge" (Scharnier), which holds the individual moments together, remains itself invisible (VI 291/237). The influence of Saussure's diacritical theory of signs is highly visible here. At the same time, the structural aspect overlaps the difference between experience and speaking; "silent experience" no longer functions one-sidedly as fundament.

2) The central locus of the formation of sense no longer lies in the region of conscious intentions, which pre-sent something, but rather in a more fundamental *process of differentiation*. "The originary explodes" (l'originaire éclate); it no longer belongs to a single type and no longer lies entirely behind us, but rather takes the form of a continual "différenciation" (VI 165/124), a "ségrégation" (VI 295/242),[16] which cannot be dealt with in terms of synthesis or receptivity.

3) The *in-between* (membrure, jointure, charnière, etc.) encompasses and overlaps the opposition between consciousness and being, subject and object, ego and alter ego, because the terms of these oppositions have no sense prior to the process of differentiation, and because the separation itself can only be thought structurally —if one does not want to content oneself with simply imputing differentiations. Merleau-Ponty speaks here of the "flesh" (chair), but he no longer means merely bodily existence; the body expands to become the "flesh of the world" (chair du monde)—a radicalization of the "bodily presence" which Husserl attributes to the things of perception.[17] The body signifies from now on the visibility and becoming-visible of the things themselves, thus, a process in which the I and the Other participate in that we ourselves belong to the world. We are of the "same stuff" as the world; Being is no longer mere in-itself, the limit to our claims to sense, but rather "element" (VI 184/139)—a suggestion of pre-Socratic thought—, *within* which we move. If there is still talk of *intentionality*, it is no longer intentionality as achievement of a representing consciousness, but "intentionality in the interior of Being" (VI 297f./244). The "intentional threads" in terms of which an intentional analysis attempts to construct the field of view are merely differentiations of a "fabric" (VI 284/231)—the metaphor of the text speaks for itself. Merleau-Ponty also appeals strongly to the model of painting, that art in which visibility itself becomes visible. The subject

loses its sovereign distance over against the things, in a sense the things view us in that they take possession of our senses, in that they fascinate us—in these descriptions Merleau-Ponty appeals to artists such as Max Ernst, Klee, Cézanne as witnesses (cf. OE 30f./167f). Spatial depth, which Merleau-Ponty already viewed as the "most 'existential' " dimension in his earlier work, since it dissolves into nothingness in the absence of a reference to our bodily Here (PP 299/256), takes an ontological turn; it is, if indeed a dimension, not the third but rather the first, since it is here that the experience of a "reversability of dimensions" congeals, the experience of a "global 'locality'—everything in the same place at the same time" (OE 56/177). The subject ceases to be the ruling center of a visual field which is ordered around him, which the Renaissance striving for a central perspective might suggest; the background character of the world cannot be dealt with in this way.

4) With the interlocking of *visible* and *invisible* we leave the ground of a philosophy which is one-sidedly concerned with presence. The invisible is not a mere not-visible (cf. ex. PP. 251/216), which is no longer seen, or not yet, or from somewhere else and by others, but rather a form of absence which as such belongs to the world. The negative is no longer a "positive which is somewhere else," but is "a true negative, i.e. an *Unverborgenheit* (unconcealment) of the *Verborgenheit* (concealment), an Urpräsentation (primal presentation) of the *Nichtpräsentierbaren* (that which cannot be presented), in other words, an originary form of the somewhere-else (originaire de l'ailleurs), a *Selbst* (self) that is an *Anderes* (Other), a hollow" (VI 308/254) (the underlined words are in German in Merleau-Ponty's writing).[18]

Accordingly, consciousness has its "blind spot," its *punctum caecum* (cf. VI 278/225, 300f./246f., 308/254); vision is itself a *not-seeing*. This means that vision is not subject to merely factual, *external* limits such as the narrowness of the visual field, which can be neutralized by changing the point of view, or such as being lost in the spectacle, which can be dealt with by a change of attitude; rather, vision has its own *inner* and fundamental limitations: in and through vision itself something is excluded; this boundary can merely be shifted by a *reorganization* of the visual field. Thus it is no longer a question of a mere incompleteness which—as Husserl would have it—moves between the poles of actual and potential, explicit and implicit. We find here a close relationship to Foucault, but also to Wittgenstein, who remarks in discussing eye and visual field: "But really you do *not* see the eye" (Tractatus 5.6). The very *idea* of a total transparency and a total fulfillment must be abandoned if sight implies a specific organization of reality. In this respect, Gestalt theory with its basic distinction of figure-ground continues to be instructive; an all-inclusive Gestalt would be a contradiction, and Merleau-Ponty thus sees a "third term between 'subject' and 'object' " in the difference figure/ground, since this "deviation" makes up perceptual sense itself and thus precedes all other differentiations (cf. VI 250/197, 300/246f.). And something similar holds for Freud's unconscious, which signifies more than the sum total of factually inaccessible representations; there is an "unconscious of consciousness" (VI 308/255).

The self-criticism which Merleau-Ponty exercises on the deficiencies in his earlier theory mentioned above are thus understandable.

The *unhappy consciousness*, which chases after something that can never be reached, is countered by a "theory of the wild spirit, which is a spirit of praxis" (VI 230/176). Cognition is no longer the search for a lost presence, an *origine perdue*, but is rather itself a creating, i.e. a process in which order arises and changes. Although this praxis, this language, just like any other, presupposes things taken for granted, making thematic is itself a mode of conduct of a higher level, and not a mere explication. But it is a good question whether or not one can still speak of a final instituting (Endstiftung) (cf. *Ibid.*).

Fluctuating determinations which remain the captive of a "bad ambiguity" are placed by encompassing points of view which in Merleau-Ponty's language are called *circularity, reversability, chiasma* or *chiasm*.[19] These are figures of reversal, which in turn recall the model of Gestalt and structure theories: re-forming and re-structuring as a change of figure and ground which does not turn into hierarchical structure.

From here we come to a new understanding of the sciences. Referring to Freud, Merleau-Ponty speaks of a necessary "mistrust of experience"; he recommends "acting as if language were not ours." The life-world is thus no longer to be understood as a "return to a pre-science (pré-science)," which would still be a counterpart of and thus itself a form of scientism, but as the challenge to grasp the "meta-scientific" and thus to win a dimension in which the results of the sciences can win sense and truth (VI 235f./181f.).

These hints and allusions will have to suffice. They ought not and cannot make Merleau-Ponty's late thought, in which influences from Saussure and Freud, Husserl and Heidegger criss-cross one another, more univocal than it is. The interpretation of Merleau-Ponty still faces a series of open tasks. The over-arching metaphor is often only a pointing, and it should be understood for what it is and not be treated as an immanent crypto-logic, for that would mean transforming that which is unfinished and contingent into something definitive, and we would end up with a cult of the fragmentary. I have merely attempted to sketch and strengthen certain lines of thought, and in closing I would merely like to underline once more just what it is that I am trying to say. Radically understood, thinking in terms of structures and Gestalt leads away from a theory in which the phenomena find their culmination in a pure *presence* for a consciousness which is *present to itself*; thought in terms of Gestalt and structure runs against the grain of a theory which is directed teleologically toward *total presence* and a *self-transparent consciousness*, even if it allows this process to taper off into infinite approximations. And this result is by no means merely negative, limiting. Is it not rather that such a "expropriation" of consciousness (SG 215/170) is advantageous for the phenomena in that it sets possibilities free which the insistence on all-embracing view—be it a last and still unattained view—traps and domesticates? Doesn't the demand for such an overview necessarily turn into a straight-jacket? Doesn't the I demand too much of itself here? Already in his earliest work Merleau-Ponty speaks of the strange possibility that the 'I think' might as it were be hallucinated by its objects (SC 239/222). The merely apparent cannot be one-sidedly reckoned to the things that we represent, it also colors our self-representations, even those of the philosopher.

What will become of a philosophy in which phenomenology runs into its limits in this manner? "Philosophy is itself only when it refuses itself the comfort of a world with a single entrance, as well as the comfort of a world with many entrances, all of which are available to the philosopher. Just like the natural man, philosophy lives at the point at which the transition from one's own self to the world and to the Other takes place, there where the paths cross" (VI 212/160). Thus, there are junctures in the net of the world where the event of sense formation draws itself together, but there is no central point from which everything is illuminated.

Translated by J. Claude Evans from the German version appearing in *Neue Entwicklungen des Phänomenologiebegriffs. Phänomenologische Forschungen* 9 (Freiburg: Alber Verlag, 1980).

NOTES

¹ cf. the translator's introduction to the German edition of *The Structure of Behavior*, IX.

² cf. *Ibid*., V ff., and Geraets 1971.

³ The fact that the return to the pre-linguistic is not the return to a pure intuitive given, but rather to pre-linguistic achievements of structuring processes, is more widely known among psychologists of language than among philosophers, who feel too at-home in the medium of language. cf. e.g. Hörmann 1978, Ch XI, XII.

⁴ Merleau-Ponty, like Scheler before him, refers to the experiments with animals by W. Köhler, Buytendijk, etc., who avoid a biologism precisely by means of differentiated structural comparisons. With regard to recent research in this field, cf. Hörmann 1978, 339 ff.

⁵ cf. Taminiaux 1976, 101 f., who sees in the *Phenomenology of Perception* a vacillation "between the notion of a return to a primary, silent consciousness, to the birthplace of sense, and that of a renewed realization of sense without any insurance in a prior grounding"; he connects this with a double interpretation and execution of the phenomenological reduction, once as "positivism" of the pre-given, and then as "art", namely as production of sense in expression. Madison (1973, 54) also speaks of an "ambiguity" in Merleau-Ponty's conception of world, which he explains in terms of the tensions within the concept of the subject.

⁶Husserl's priority of the Ego over against the Other—and be it in the sublime form of a primal-Ego—is based on the fact that the bodily present appears here in its fundamental form (cf. de-presentification (Ent-Gegenwärtigung) as a-lienation (Ent-Fremdung), Hua. VI, 189).

⁷ Cf. Beaufret's comments on Merleau-Ponty's lecture "The Primacy of Perception", held in 1946 (152 f.), where Beaufret objects against holding on to an idealistic vocabulary. cf. also Foucault's later critique of a mixed form of transcendental philosophy and anthropology, where man is presented as a strange "empirical-transcendental doublet" (1966, 239 ff.), and Derrida's similar critique of an anthropologizing of phenomenology ("Les find de l'homme", in: 1972, 129 ff.).

⁸ For the connection between the understanding of the body and of history, cf. Métraux 1976.

⁹ Blankenburg too sees the dialectical view of sickness to be characterized by the fact that a change in the frame of reference is reckoned with and that the *standards* of the patient as well as those of the therapist are set in motion.

¹⁰ cf. Husserl, Hua. III, § 106: Negation as well as affirmation presuppose a prior "position."

¹¹ When Husserl later increasingly returns to a preobjective stratum of the constitution of sense, the question shifts to another level.

¹² This is more than an analogy, if one recalls that the recognition of forms is subject to rules; recall the efforts toward a semiotics of perception.

¹³ Merleau-Ponty makes a similar distinction with reference to attention (cf. PP 38/29-30).

¹⁴ cf. Waldenfels, 1977. In addition, with regard to the limits of codifying the speech situation, Hörmann 1978, Ch. XI: "The knowledge which might be codified is based on an *ability* which is not codified" (325).

¹⁵ With regard to the convergences with structural linguistics and structuralism, cf.

Lanigan 1972, Fontaine-De Visscher 1974, Kockelmans 1976, Waldenfels 1976, Gregori 1977; to the relations to structural ethnology cf. Merleau-Ponty: "De Mauss à Lévi-Strauss" (SG 132 ff./114 ff); to the renewed concern for Freud cf. Merleau-Ponty's Forward to Hesnard, also Frostholm 1978.

[16] cf. already PP 22 f./15f.: with regard to the "ségrégation du champ"; here, as in many other cases, it is impossible to overlook continuities or at least correspondences in all shifts of point of view.

[17] "When we say that the perceived thing is grasped 'in person' or 'in the flesh' (*leibhaft*), this is to be taken literally: the flesh of what is perceived, this compact particle which stops exploration, and this optimum which terminates it all reflect my own incarnation and are its counterpart" (SG 211/167).

[18] The metaphor of a "hollow" (creux) or a "fold" (pli) in Being, in opposition to that of a "hole in Being", which is ascribed to Hegel, appears early in Merleau-Ponty's writing, initially tied up with the defense against consciousness as pure negativity (cf. SC 136 f./127 f., PP 249/215).

[19] Merleau-Ponty found the figurative use of the term "chiasma" (literally: the intercrossing of the optic nerves) in Valéry, who used it to refer to the exchange of glances between two corporeal beings (cf. SG 294/231).

Bibliography*

1. Works by Merleau-Ponty

La structure du comportement. Paris 1949 (= SC). English by Alden L. Fisher: *The Structure of Behavior.* (Boston: Beacon Press, 1963). German by Bernhard Waldenfels: *Die Struktur des Verhaltens.* Berlin, 1976.

Phénoménologie de la perception. Paris, 1945 (= PP). English by Colin Smith: *The Phenomenology of Perception.* (London: Routledge & Kegan Paul, 1962).

"Le primat de la perception et ses conséquences philosophiques," in: *Bulletin de la Société Française de Philosophie,* 41, 1947, Pp. 119-153. English translation by James Edie: "The Primacy of Perception", in *The Primacy of Perception.* (Evanston: Northwestern University Press, 1964).

Eloge de la philosophie. Paris, 1953 (= EP). English by James Edie & John Wild: *In Praise of Philosophy.* (Evanston: Northwestern University Press, 1963).

Les aventures de la dialectique. Paris, 1955. English by Joseph Bien: *Adventures of the Dialectic.* (Evanston: Northwestern University Press, 1973).

Signes. Paris, 1960 (= SG). English by Richard C. McCleary: *Signs.* (Evanston: Northwestern University Press, 1964).

Forward to A, Hesnard: *L'oeuvre de Freud et son importance dans le monde moderne.* Paris, 1960.

"Un inédit de M. Merleau-Ponty", in *Revue de métaphysique et de morale,* 67, 1962, Pp. 401-409. English in: *The Primacy of Perception.*

*When the page number is given twice, the number before the slash refers to the French original, the number after the slash to the English translation.

L'oeil et l'esprit. Paris (= OE). English in: *The Primacy of Perception.*
Le visible et l'invisible. Paris, 1964 (= VI). English by Alfonso Lingis: *The Visible and the Invisible.* (Evanston: Northwestern University Press, 1969).

2. Additional Literature

Blankenburg, W. "Wie weit reicht die dialektische Betrachtungsweise in der Psychiatrie?" (Unpublished manuscript).

Derrida, J. *Marges de la philosophie.* Paris, 1972.

Fontaine-De Visscher, L. *Phénoméne ou structure? Essai sur le langage chez Merleau-Ponty.* Brussels, 1974.

Foucault, M. *Les mots et les choses.* Paris, 1966. English: *The Order of Things.* (Pantheon, 1970).

Frostholm, B. *Leib und Unbewußtes. Freuds Begriff des Unbewußten interpretiert durch den Leib-Begriff Merleau-Pontys.* Bonn, 1978.

Geraets, T. F. *Vers une nouvelle philosophie transcendantale. La genèse de la philosophie de M. Merleau-Ponty jusqu'à la "Phènoménologie de la perception."* The Haag, 1971.

Grathoff, R. & Sprondel, W. (ed.). *Merleau-Ponty und das Problem der Struktur in den Sozialwissenschaften.* Stuttgart, 1976.

Gregori, I. *Merleau-Pontys Phänomenologie der Sprache.* Heidelberg, 1977.

Gurwitsch, A. *The Field of Consciousness.* (Pittsburgh: Dusquesne University Press, 1976).

Hörmann, H. *Meinen und Verstehen. Grundzüge einer psychologischen Semantik.* Frankfurt, 1978.

Kockelmans, J. J. "Strukturalismus und existenziale Phänomenologie," in: Grathoff & Sprondel 1976.

Lanigan, R. L. *Speaking and Semiology. Merleau-Ponty's Phenomenological Theory of Existential Communication.* (The Haag: Martinus Nijhoff, 1972).

Madison, G. B. *La phénoménologie de Merleau-Ponty.* Paris, 1973.

Métraux, A. "Über Leiblichkeit und Geschichtlichkeit als Konstituentien der Sozialphilosophie Merleau-Pontys," in Grathoff & Sprondel 1976.

Plügge, H. *Der Mensch und sein Leib.* Tübingen, 1967.

Taminiaux, J. "Über Erfahrung, Ausdruck und Struktur: ihre Entwicklung in der Phänomenologie Merleau-Pontys," in Grathoff & Sprondel 1976.

Waldenfels, B. "Das Problem der Leiblichkeit bei Merleau-Ponty," *Philosophisches Jahrbuch,* 75, 1968, Pp. 347-365.

--------- "Die Offenheit sprachlicher Strukturen bei Merleau-Ponty," in: Grathoff & Sprondel 1976.

--------- "Verhaltensnorm und Verhaltenskontext," in: Waldenfels, B. et. al. (eds.), *Phänomenologie und Marxismus,* Vol. 2, Frankfurt, 1977.

--------- *Der Spielraum des Verhaltens.* Frankfurt 1980 (includes the articles 1968, *1976, 1977).*

The Meaning And Development Of Merleau-Ponty's Concept Of Structure

JAMES M. EDIE
Northwestern University

Much of the most recent commentary on Merleau-Ponty's work concerns the development of his concept of structure and structuralism.[1] Many of the most recent commentators are particularly interested in revealing the common thread which they claim runs through his thought on structuralism from his earliest work to the end. These commentators nearly all divide Merleau-Ponty's development into three periods. It is the thesis of this paper that we need to distinguish four very distinct periods in his development on this question and, secondly, that the theories of structure developed in these four different periods are so distinct from one another as to be the possible bases for four completely distinct philosophical methodologies. It is my thesis that it is only during the third period (what I have elsewhere called the "middle" period) that he developed his ideas on linguistic structuralism in any strict sense.

Though there is an interest in language from his earliest works (*The Structure of Behavior* and *The Phenomenology of Perception*), there is no discussion of structuralism in the technical sense. It was only after the appearance of Sartre's book *What is Literature?* in 1947 that Merleau-Ponty's thought began to focus almost exclusively on language and linguistics.[2] In 1948 he gave an extensive first course on language at Lyon, a course that was repeated in much developed form at the Sorbonne in 1949 under the title *Consciousness and the Acquisi-*

tion of Language. During the following decade he was drawn more and more into the theory of language and literature. With his typical thoroughness he began with a survey of all the material then available on scientific linguistics, with special reference to Saussure. Thus, unlike his contemporaries in the Anglo-American philosophical world, who developed a theory of language based on speech-acts (Wittgenstein, Austin, Ryle, etc.) which totally ignores the contributions of scientific linguistics, Merleau-Ponty's reflections on language are based directly on linguistic structuralism. During the period from 1949 to 1953, the year of his inaugural lecture at the Collège de France, his interest in language is almost exclusive. As I have said elsewhere: from 1949 onward language began to become his central preoccupation; it was no longer treated as just one example among many of the specifically human institution of meaning, but is now set up as the privileged mode of our experience of meaning of all kinds. The structures of perception, and even gestalt presentations are interpreted in terms of the oppositive, diacritical binary oppositions of phonology. Even color perception is seen to be a matter of being immersed in a system of differences, analogous to those of language. In short, from being a peripheral, though always important, consideration in his phenomenological investigations, *the analysis of language now takes the central place.* In his inaugural address to the Collège de France in 1953 he went so far as to credit Saussurean linguistics with developing a "theory of signs" that could serve as a sounder basis for the philosophy of history than the thought of either Marx or Hegel, which he had primarily adopted in the works of his "pre-linguistic" period. He did not, of course, believe (like Wittgenstein) that the study of language alone would solve all philosophical problems, but he did believe that linguistics would give us the paradigm model on the basis of which he would be able to elaborate a theory of the human sciences and thus establish a universal, philosophical anthropology.[3]

However, from the commencement of his teachings at the Collège de France he begins to doubt this new position and his thought begins to move into a new and strikingly different direction. From this year, 1953, he seems to have lost interest both in *The Prose of the World*, the book on which he was then working, and his project for a book on *The Origin of Truth*, and had completely abandoned all interest in both these projects by 1959.[4] The reasons for this abrupt and puzzling change of direction are obscure though I will present my own hypothesis below. In any case it is evident that the fourth and final period of his thought, which begins around 1959, culminated in the difficult and obscure reflections of *The Visible and the Invisible*, a work which was meant to replace all the projects he had begun during the 1953-1959 period.

I. MERLEAU-PONTY AND LINGUISTIC STRUCTURALISM.

As I have said, I distinguish four periods in the development of Merleau-Ponty's concept of structure. These can be conveniently labeled: (1) Gestaltist, (2) Dialectical, (3) Structuralist, and (4) Post-Structuralist (in a specifically Merleau-Pontean, i.e. pre-Derridian, sense of "post-structuralism"). For the purpose of our discussion here it is best to begin with Merleau-Ponty's most highly developed discussions of structuralism and then return to his earliest work before going on to the final period.

His discovery of linguistic structuralism, he tells us, was primarily influenced by Saussure's theory of the linguistic sign.

> We have learned from Saussure that, taken singly, signs do not signify anything, and that each one of them does not so much express a meaning as mark a divergence of meaning between itself and other signs.[5]
> The well-known definition of the sign as "diacritical, oppositive, and negative" means that language is present in the speaking subject as a system of intervals between signs and significations, and that, as a unity, the act of speech simultaneously operates the differentiation of these two orders.[6]

In short, the scientific study of phonology shows us that natural languages are based on systems of binary oppositions according to which the recognized phonemes of a given language are opposable, according to rule, to all the other phonemes of that language. The "miracle" of language is that a restricted number of phonemes—which in themselves mean nothing—enable us to develop the whole world of discourse based on a highly restricted number of binary oppositions which provide us with the fundamental, formal rules of our language.

At the same time, and not surprisingly in view of his earlier phenomenology, it is not this aspect of linguistic theory which most interested Merleau-Ponty or held his attention. He was even less interested (until he was forced to face it in *The Prose of the World*) in the distinction between surface and depth grammar and, indeed, tried to avoid for as long as he could any notion of an "ideal grammar" underlying the surface string.[7] We will take up the reasons for this presently. For now, let us emphasize that one distinction which Merleau-Ponty took from Saussure, namely the distinction between *la langue* and *la parole*, *la langue* being the *rules* of language and *la parole* being the *acts* of speaking.

(1) First, in his course of 1949, *Consciousness and the Acquisition of Language*, *la langue* is defined as "a system of possibilities" whereas *la parole* is "what one says." *La langue* would therefore define the field of ideal possibilities for expression and *la parole* would be the exercise of these possibilities. The dialectical difficulty—and this is what most fascinates Merleau-Ponty—with this distinction is that *la langue* itself follows a "kind of blundering logic" rather than the purely conceptual logic of the proposition. *La langue* is to speech as what the body is to consciousness. The body, like language, follows a "blind logic" which presents us with a "conventional" or "cultural" system which is not based on any explicit common decision. We cannot, for instance, give an exact date to the time when the Latin language became French though, as we follow the diachronic evolution of this language, we may be able to note the emergence over time of a certain "archetectonic" which is no longer that of Latin. The unity of the system is not that of an ideal grammar, in Merleau-Ponty's view, but of "the idea of a unity of a language-function across languages...of a concrete universality which realizes itself only gradually and finds itself treating the expressive desire which animates languages rather than the transitory forms which are its result."[8] French defines itself in the present as the common aim of all subjects who speak it to the extent that they are able to communicate among themselves. Language, therefore, is neither "a transcendent reality with respect to all the speaking subjects" nor is it "a phantasm formed by the individual."[9] It is rather the enigmatic point of intersection of speaking and meaning which enables thought to be articulated.[10] As Vendryes said: "Language is an ideal which can be sought, but never found; a potential reality never actually realized; a becoming which never comes."[11] The importance of structuralist linguistics for Merleau-Ponty is to have put this problem at the center though how it is to be solved, at this stage, is unclear.

(2) In the section on "Linguistics" in his essay on *Phenomenology and the Sciences of Man* (1951) Merleau-Ponty is more dramatic: "But for the subject who is actually speaking, who is no longer an *observer* confronting language as an *object*, his language is undoubtedly a distinct reality. There are regions where he can make himself understood and others where he cannot.... the circumstances may be more or less precise, more or less rigorous, more or less com-

plex, depending upon the culture of the speaker. But for him there is always a moment, a boundary, beyond which he no longer understands and is no longer understood."[12]

Clearly, Merleau-Ponty understands *la langue* exclusively in terms of what linguists today call the "surface string" as opposed to "deep structures." But, even so, *la langue* prescribes the common rules according to which all must speak if they are to be understood; language in this sense is correlative to and co-extensive with acts of speaking. Language is not a thing but a system of rules which subsists "in the air *between* the speaking subjects but never fully realized in any of them."[13]

For the members of any natural linguistic community present usage is independent of etymology and the past history of the language. The speaking subject is turned towards the future. Language is the intention of saying something about something to somebody. No matter how "scientific" we may become there is "no rigorous procedure which will enable us to determine the exact beginning of a linguistic reality. It has no precise spatial and temporal limits...[There is] no determinate place where Provençal as a whole is perfectly realized... [in fact] there is only one single language, since there is no way of finding the precise limit where one passes into another."[14]

> The language which is present, actual, and effective becomes the model for understanding other possible modes of speech. It is in our experience of speaking that we must find the germ of universality which will enable us to understand other languages.[15]

Thus, in his discussions of the distinction between *la langue* and *la parole* Merleau-Ponty throughout seems to give priority to *la parole* which can only lead to difficulties when he later attempts to stress the systematic and formal character of "sign systems" as he does in *In Praise of Philosophy* (1953). There he writes, in a passage which is much more in the strictly structuralist vein while retaining his usual rhetorical eloquence:

> Meaning lies latent not only in language, in political and religious institutions, but in modes of kinship, in machines, in the landscape, in production, and, in general, in all the modes of human commerce. An interconnection among all these phenomena is possible, *since they are all symbolisms*, and perhaps even the translation of one symbolism into another is possible.[16]

(3) It was, indeed, in this inaugural lecture of 1953 that Merleau-Ponty summed up the central focus of his interest in scientific linguistic structuralism:

> The theory of signs as developed in linguistics...implies a conception of historical meaning which gets beyond the opposition of *things* versus *consciousness*. Living language is precisely that togetherness of thinking and thing which causes the difficulty. In the act of speaking, the subject, in his tone and in his style, bears witness to his autonomy, since nothing is more proper to him, and yet at the same moment, and without contradiction, he is turned toward the linguistic community and is dependent on his language. The will to speak is one and the same as the will to be understood. The presence of the individual in an institution and of the institution in the individual is evident in the case of linguistic change. It is often the wearing down of a form which suggests to us a new way of using the means of discrimination which are present in the language at a given time. The constant need for communication leads us to invent and accept a new usage which is not deliberate and yet which is systematic. The contingent fact, taken over by the will to expression, becomes a new means of expression which takes its place, and has a lasting sense in the history of this language. In such cases, there is a rationality in the contingent, a lived logic, a self-constitution of which we have definite need in trying to understand the union of contingency and meaning in history...[17]

Readers of *The Visible and the Invisible* will not fail to foresee here the developments which later lead Merleau-Ponty to give up his attempt to use the structural analysis of language as the privileged method and model for the explanation of *all* experience and to re-insert it into experience as just one more manifestation of something more fundamental, namely the unity of *thing* and *consciousness* in some ineffable, inarticulable, unity which transcends all contradictions.

In short, what most interested Merleau-Ponty in the structuralist attempt to establish phonological, morphological and syntactical rules (which we call *la langue*) *according to which* we must speak in order to make sense, is the dialectual relationship of these rules or structures to actual acts of usage. On the one hand the structures of language are nothing other than the scientific description of speech acts, and therefore are ontologically dependent on a community of speakers.

On the other hand this community of speakers must already—in some dumb, sub-understood manner—follow the rules of *la langue* even while their language patterns are being described. Here we have a good dialectical situation. Neither is prior to the other, neither can subsist without the other, neither is independent of the other. Each is necessary for the constitution of meaning and the articulation of thought. It is, I submit, Merleau-Ponty's attempt at a dialectical reconciliation of these two aspects of language which is at once the high point of his reflections on linguistic structuralism and at the same time the ruination of his structuralist-linguistic program. For, no sooner is this dialectical problem carefully stated—and it is stated again and again in the works of this period—than Merleau-Ponty abandons it. But before continuing our argument we must return to Merleau-Ponty's pre-structualist writings. I divide his conceptions in this period under two headings: the Gestaltist, and the Dialectical.

II. MERLEAU-PONTY'S EARLY THEORIES OF STRUCTURE.

To bring a dialectical cast, even of exposition, to the phenomenological thought of Edmund Husserl would seem to be an audacious enterprise—given the fact both that the name of Hegel and the term "dialectic" are excluded from the writings of Husserl, by conscious design. From the very first pages of the *Phenomenology of Perception* we are clearly in a new and strange phenomenological climate. But before going to the *Phenomenology of Perception* it is necessary to take a brief look at Merleau-Ponty's first major work, namely *The Structure of Behavior*, to examine the sense that he gives to the word "structure" there. The major source of the notion of structure developed in Merleau-Ponty's first book is that which was developed in Gestalt psychology, which in turn was largely influenced by Husserl's *Third Investigation*, "The Logic of Parts and Wholes." This is the notion which defines the structure as being more than a simple combination of parts or elements, but rather the new reality which emerges from the special form in which a number of necessarily interdependent parts or elements combine in such wise that the whole would not be what it is if it were composed of different elements, nor would the elements which constitute a given whole be the same if they were to be found in a different whole or in isolation.

Whether one takes the route of conceptual analysis, as Husserl did in the *Third Investigation*, or bases oneself on the empirical results of Gestalt psychology, as Merleau-Ponty preferred to do, there are essentially two ways in which parts and wholes can be related. (1) There are wholes which are mere "aggregates," constituted of parts or element which have no intrinsic connection with one another, no *reason* residing in themselves to be "taken together." (2) And then there are other "wholes" whose analysis into parts shows that the parts mutually interpenetrate one another and logically imply one another.

This latter serves as the basis for the notion of "structure" developed by such German thinkers as Rubin, Lewin, Metzgar, Koffka, Koehler, Gelb, Goldstein, and Gurwitsch. After Gurwitsch fled Germany in 1933 and established himself in Paris, Merleau-Ponty became his student and collaborator.[18] The bibliography with which Gurwitsch provided him, particularly in his famous article "Quelques aspects...de la psychologie de la forme," serves as the backbone for the investigations in *The Structure of Behavior*, even though Merleau-Ponty hardly recognizes the important influence of Gurwitsch on this book and on his thought as a whole. On the basis of this Gestaltist literature and the analyses it contains, Merleau-Ponty, in *The Structure of Behavior*, reinterprets the distinction between "the physical," "the biological," and "the mental" to show that biological (or vital) structures presuppose physical structures, and that mental structures presuppose both. They are not only *de facto* but *logically* cumulative in such wise that the higher, though it can never be reduced to the lower, necessary presupposes it. Hegel is hardly mentioned in this book; the entire analysis and argument is based, usually indirectly and through Gestalt theory, on Husserl's concept of *Fundierung*, an analysis of how higher forms of experience can be and necessarily must be *founded* on lower forms.

This early notion of structure is clearly not to be identified with that of linguistic structuralism, though interesting analogies can be formulated. There is certainly no evidence that the founders of linguistic structuralism, like Troubetskoy, Saussure, Jakobson, or their followers, were particularly influenced by Gestalt psychology (though they were influenced by Husserl's *Logical Investigations*). Their notion of structuralism arose quite independently of any psychological research. Nevertheless, later on, when Merleau-Ponty does develop his views on linguistic structuralism he finds it perfectly natural to describe language as "not a Gestalt of the moment, but a Gestalt in movement, evolving toward a certain equilibrium."[19]

What distinguishes the structure of the diachronic natural language from that of the Gestaltists is that the elements constituting the "structure" are not simply and statically *juxtaposed* but are dynamically developing in time. It is clear that anyone who would identify these two senses of structure would be making a serious equivocation. Raymond Boudon has rightly insisted on this point. However, it does not seem that he is fully justified in his extremely negative criticism of what might be taken to be the fumbling of Merleau-Ponty's early work. He writes in one place of Merleau-Ponty and Goldstein as follows:

Merleau-Ponty's early work. He writes in one place of Merleau-Ponty and Goldstein as follows:

> Even though at their time the works of Merleau-Ponty and the French translation of *The Organism* were able to appear as revelations, one does not find in either of them any kind of theory of the organism or of behavior *as systems*, but only a passionately interesting collection of observations. No doubt these obervations show that an organism reacts as a whole and that a behavior cannot be understood except as a whole. But who could ever have doubted such banalities?[20]

There is a certain fluidity, lack of contour, perhaps a deliberate inexactitude, vagueness, and ambiguity in Merleau-Ponty's early definition of structure, but it does not seem that the originality of his work can be summarily dismissed. On the other hand it is clear that, as Merleau-Ponty developed, he radically changed his definition of "structure" at each step.

In any case what is added in Merleau-Ponty's second major work, *The Phenomenology of Perception*, is a new and different concept of "structure"—a notion greatly influenced by his own idiosyncratic reading of Hegel. What distinguishes *The Phenomenology of Perception* from Merleau-Ponty's first book is the highly dialectical style of exposition it employs (something nowhere found in *The Structure of Behavior*). Though Merleau-Ponty continues to speak the language of Husserl and Gurwitsch in developing the eidetic structures of perceptual consciousness, and its embodiment, his writing takes on a very heavy Hegelian tone—something which Husserl would certainly have disavowed. Moreover, and secondly, when he treats of language in this book, there is no mention of Saussure or of structural linguistics. He is still completely innocent of these authors. Language is treated as but one aspect of the total bodily organization in the primary field of experience as one more aspect of the expressive and gestural constitution of meaning which Merleau-Ponty orchestrates in this book.[21]

The dialectical cast of his interpretation of Husserlian phenomenology is evident from the first sentences of the Introduction. He gives a "Hegelian" interpretation of the four central concepts of Husserl's phenomenology: namely, the concept of "the reduction to experience, of the experience of other persons in "transcendental intersubjectivity," the notions of fact and essence, and the notion of intentionality. The phenomenological reduction, we read, is both possible and impossible at one and the same time; there is a truth of solipsism and a truth of intersubjectivity and both must be maintained in their opposed balance. Every fact is the instantiation of an essence and yet no fact can exhaust the essence; the world of experience can both be known and at the same time not known, eidetically. Consciousness is a "project of the world" which transcends itself towards what is is not and never will be, and consciousness is, at the same time, the "pre-objective" possession of itself in immanence. Consciousness, in short, is both transcendent and immanent, at the same time.

It seems that Merleau-Ponty took his notion of dialectics from two major sources, first of all from the teaching of Kojève, whose specialized and "existential" interpretation of Hegel made the members of Merleau-Ponty's student-generation for the first time fully conversant with Hegel. Merleau-Ponty is strongly influenced by the strong equivocation which pervades Kojève's interpretation insofar as he seems almost to identify the sense of "phenomenology" in *The Phenomenology of Mind* with Husserl's phenomenology. This bringing together of Husserl and Hegel as contributors to *one* new kind of phenomenology is characteristic of the French phenomenology not only of Merleau-Ponty but also of Sartre.

The second source of Merleau-Ponty's dialectical notions comes mostly from Marx, and was no doubt highly influenced by his leftist political interests and his special interest in the philosophy of history and culture.

He wrote in *Sense and Nonsense*:

> ...all the great philosophical ideas of the past century—the philosophy of Marx and Nietzsche, phenomenology, German existentialism, and psychoanalysis—had their beginnings in Hegel; it was he who started the attempt to explore the irrational integrated into an expanded reason which remains the task of our century. He is the inventor of that Reason, broader than the understanding, which can respect the variety and singularity of individual consciousness, civilization, ways of thinking, and historical contingency but which nevertheless does not give up the attempt to master them in order to guide to their own truth.[22]

In the light of this and similarly strong statements on the importance of Hegel's dialectical method it is all the more impressive to note, once again, that in 1953—with his discovery of linguistic structuralism—he states that the Saussurean theory of the sign will supplant both Marx and Hegel. Thus we cannot doubt that, in the development of his own thought, there is a strong contrast between Merleau-Ponty's earliest concepts of structure and those we have presented as the discoveries of the years 1947-1953 when he dedicated himself to an enthusiasm for linguistics which, at least in its verbal expression, as well as in its fate in his future thought, sometimes seems embarrassing. There are clearly themes and ideas which go through Merleau-Ponty's corpus as a whole—ideas which come up again and again in different guises. There is thus a "unity" to his project as a whole. What is, however, not unified and completely distinct are the four senses of "structure" and the four methods he developed to deal with it at each of the four turning-points of his career.

III. MERLEAU-PONTY'S FINAL, POST-STRUCTURALIST, PERIOD.

Given the strength of his convictions concerning the importance of linguistic structuralism for the explanation of human behavior and all that he wrote about the matter in the decade 1949-1959, it is puzzling to all of his readers that he should have so abruptly and completely abandoned this structuralism in his final work. As we have noted he left *The Prose of the World* incomplete, and totally abandoned his plan to write on *The Origin of Truth*—which was to have been, in his own words, the crown of his philosophical career.[23] Instead, from around 1959 until the time of his death he began working on a series of studies now entitled *The Visible and the Invisible*. This work, far from ever having been completed,[24] comes down to us in the form of a half-written treatise—directed mainly against Sartrean ontology—and an unfinished and disordered mass of working notes. For better or for worse there are a number of contemporary writers who take the development of the ideas in *The Visible and the Invisible* to be a rectilinear development and final culmination of the major thrust of his work from the very beginning. Some of these writers go further to find a thread which unites Merleau-Ponty's thought as it developed through these various stages in terms of what they call a "structural onotology." It does not seem to me that this can be correct for the simple reason that the sense of "structure" which one can glean from a reading of *The Visible and the Invisible* has only a tenuous relationship to his earlier notions. Two points must be made.

(1) The first point concerns Merleau-Ponty's dialectical method which is more and more emphasized, and which becomes more and more obscure as his work on *The Visible and the Invisible* progresses. About the only thing that is truly clear is that in his concept of dialectic, unlike that of Hegel but like that of Sartre,[25] there is no room for and no necessity of any dialectical reconciliation between opposites, in short no *synthesis*. His is a dialectic which holds contradictories together in a never stable and always temporally evolving disequilibrium. Always the "philosopher of ambiguity," in his final period Merleau-Ponty becomes the philosopher of contradiction.

Any commentator who adopts as a heuristic principle the rule that one must explain the obscure passages in an author by the passages on the same subject in which he expresses himself clearly, will not attempt to interpret his early works, whether inspired by Gestalt psychology, by dialectics, or by linguistic structuralism, in terms of the argumentation of *The Visible and the Invisible*,[26] for this would be to interpret what is clearly said by what is obscure and, ultimately, to give no interpretation at all. For, it is not at all evident that the guiding principle for the interpretation of the thought of a philosopher ought to be that his thought improves, matures, and gets better as he grows older. If such a principle were to be universally adopted, we would find ourselves interpreting Kant's *Critique of Pure Reason* in terms of the obscure, mystical ravings of the *Opus Posthumum*. There is certainly no apriori reason to suppose that the rambling and sometimes incoherent positions taken in the working notes of *The Visible and the Invisible* ought to be granted a special place in the interpretation of Merleau-Ponty's thought as a whole.

(2) This brings us to the second and more important point, namely that of an interpretation of the "binary" yet "dialectical" opposition of the "visible" and the "invisible," which he says pervades and constitutes the entire field of "Being."

It is not clear that the various oppositions which Merleau-Ponty sets up binding and dividing the "visible" and the "invisible" together are dialectical, at least in the Hegelian sense. It would seem more just to interpret them like a Heraclitean identification of opposites held together in their contradictoriness at one and the same time.

When we first begin to make a list of the things Merleau-Ponty means by the "visible"and the "invisible" we are reassured that they should be able to be phenomenologically elucidated:

1. The perception of objects which are not, strictly speaking, given to me in perceptual presentation, but which I

nevertheless perceive, such as "objects behind my back."
2. The experience of imagining absences, possibilities, potentialities, contingencies, counter-factual conditionals, the subjunctive, the optative, etc.
3. The perception of others insofar as the perception of the other presents a body (surface) in which there is a (non-spatial) mind, the body being "visible," the mind being "invisible" (in the sense of the Husserlian appresented object). The experience of my own mind in my own body which is "posterior" to the experience of embodiment.
4. The silence which surrounds language, as *la langue* "precedes" and surrounds *la parole*.[27]
5. Consciousness and Unconsciousness.
6. The Husserlian distinction between fact and essence.
7. The relationship between the present state of a science which is moving towards a more perfect stage of the same science, which will be recognizably the *same* science, though it does not yet exist.
Etc.

If this were all that Merleau-Ponty meant by the opposition of the"visible" and the "invisible," we could all heave a sigh of relief, for we are on familiar ground. And, no doubt, he does have a universal synthesis of such oppositions in mind and wants to show forth their "ground." The question, then, is about the methodology for reaching this ground or ultimate foundation (in "Being" with a capital *B*). It certainly is not Gestaltist; it certainly is not phenomenological; it certainly is not structuralist; is it dialectical?

Much has been written about this and, in the absence of a full study of the development of Merleau-Ponty's concept of dialectics, we must limit ourselves to a few observations. The Being which is revealed by this dialectic is a Being which is never wholly itself, that is what it is, and thus is the foundation of its own truth and meaning [there is *no distinction* between meaning and truth in Merleau-Ponty by this time] but whose meaning and truth transcend it. Its internal relations are both *necessary* and *incompatible*.

> An absolute negativism—that is, one that thinks the negative is its originality—and an absolute positivism—that is, one that thinks being in its plenitude and its self-sufficiency—are exactly synonymous; there is not the least divergence between them.[28]

When one suggests that, in his final period, Merleau-Ponty may have ushered in the age of "post-structuralism," one evokes the frightening thought of Derridianism, and one must be fair. But the central question such thinkers, including Merleau-Ponty must be held to answer is whether their sense of dialectics—unlike the classical sense—requires not only the abandonment of any theory of the transcendental presuppositions of formal logic (since there can no longer be a transcendental, i.e. experiential, foundation of anything) but of formal logic itself. We have learned in contemporary debate that the most instructive question which can be posed to a person who professes to hold a dialectical logic is whether or not this dialectical logic supplants and erases the need for a formal logic. If the answer is "yes," we know the man is not only not a very good logician, but that he is also not a very good Platonist or Hegelian. Certainly the Derridian post-structuralists and deconstructionists speak and write in this manner,[29] and it is for this reason that one can, in reading Merleau-Ponty's final work, pose the question of his responsibility for it.

However, in all fairness to Merleau-Ponty, we must note that one of the difficulties in reading his last work is that, except when he is arguing with Sartre, he makes very few theoretical claims at all. Instead, we have a plethora of fascinating examples, cast up in a prolific and often chaotic profusion: Since each individual perceives his own world, the common world (*koinos kosmos*) is not perceived; yet, still, it is perceived. My hand has to be felt from the inside at the same time it is felt from the outside, and seeing is also a kind of touching of things with our look. The body sees the world but it also experiences itself being seen by things—the experience of painters, in which Merleau-Ponty was so interested—to the point that one is no longer able to say who sees and who is seen.

> . . . it is not I who sees, not *he* who sees, because an anonymous visibility inhabits both of us, a vision in general, in virtue of that primordial property that belongs to the flesh, being here and now, of radiating everywhere and forever, being an individual, of being also . . universal.[30]

Until we reach what could be, or could have been, the culminating apostrophe of his final thought:

> There is an experience of the visible thing as pre-existing my vision, but this experience is not a fusion, a coincidence; because my eyes which see, my hands which touch, can also be seen and touched, because, therefore, in

> this sense they see and touch the visible, the tangible, from within . . . . the world and I are within one another and there is no anteriority of the *percipere* over the *percipi*, there is simultaneity or even retardation.[31]

No philosopher of experience can help but stand in awe of Merleau-Ponty's uncanny ability to describe the fine nuances of perceptual experience, an ability in this regard greater even than that of William James. *It is the philosophical method behind it that is in question.* What are we to make of these statements methodologically? Is this dialectical argument? Is "anteriority" in this passage to be understood in a logical sense? In a temporal sense? In an ontological sense? Answers to questions of this kind appear nowhere. One thing is certain: if there is no "anteriority" of the *percipere* in *any* sense, we have abandoned phenomenology. No matter that the "there is" of Being can be called "the intersection of being," "reversibility," "chiasm," "flesh," even "savage flesh." It is not that these metaphors cannot be understood or that they are not extremely (often misleadingly) evocative. But what is the (philosophical) *method* for the investigation of this "Being"? Can it be called "structuralist" in any sense that will yield a "structural ontology"? Though some commentators say so, it is not clear that Merleau-Ponty does

IV. CONCLUSION.

But to the extent that we are mainly interested in the *evolution* and *development* of his thought, we are not so much interested in the question of whether or not his last work involves either a return to an earlier concept of dialectics, or the development of a new concept. Albert Rabil[32] tells us that during the years 1945-50 (therefore, though Rabil does not say so, during the period of his discovery of linguistic structuralism) Merleau-Ponty decided to abandon his earlier "dialectic." Whether or not this is true we are not certain, and must propose a hypothesis. The main question we are interested in here is *why* certainly after 1959, and perhaps as early as 1953, he abandoned all work on *The Prose of the World* and took up the obscure reflections which finally emerged in *The Visible and the Invisible.*

My hypothesis is based on an examination of those passages in *The Prose of the World* in which, in spite of himself, Merleau-Ponty is required by the logic of his own investigations into language to recognize and find a place for the algorithmic and formally logical structures of language.[33] If, of course, he had been able to study the (later) linguistics of scholars like Zellig Harris or Noam Chomsky, instead of the much more primitive and undeveloped literature available to him, he would not, perhaps, have been so long able to ignore the universal apriori structures of deep grammar or spend so much argument attempting to show that the *only* "universal" characteristics of language come about from the "oblique passage," or the "lateral transfer" that occurs between one surface structure and another.

Certainly, it would seem that the kind of binary logic presupposed in the very foundations of phonology and linguistic structuralism in general, the only logic the computer can use, the only logic in which linguists like Chomsky, for instance, would be interested, is too closely dependent on the law of non-contradiction as it is formulated in formal logic (as well as in the transcendental critique of formal logic)[34] for Merleau-Ponty to find it congenial.

It is as if he came to see this pitfall of linguistic structuralism only little by little. It is as if when, finally forced by a deeper reading of structural linguistics, he saw tht he was going to have to abandon or modify his earlier "Gestaltist" and "dialectical" interpretation of linguistic structuralism, he abandoned it. Not much more can be said. There are those, like myself, who (since we believe the method of linguistic structuralism will provide us with a model and method for explanation in the human sciences with far more explanatory power than any method presently in use) would have found a further and newer development of Merleau-Ponty's structuralism a positive advance in his thought. There are no doubt others who find his return to or creation of an opposed "dialectical" method an advance also. The important point in either case requires the recognition of the shifting senses in which he used the term "structure" in the various periods of his philosophical development and the recognition that there is no rectilinear development of any single, clearly delineated and well-defined concept of structure or structuralism which runs through his thought from beginning to end.

NOTES

[1]The most recent, authoritative and complete discussion of this literature is in: Klaus Boer, *Maurice Merleau-Ponty—Die Entwicklung seines Strukturdenkens* (Bonn: Bouvier) 1978. Boer gives an almost complete bibliography with interpretative discussion of a high order. Though I disagree with his central thesis—which is opposed in what I write below—his discussion is to be highly recommended. I intend to devote a subsequent article to a more minute examination of his own viewpoint. In this study I

am treating the general current tendency, of which he is the best example, in Merleau-Ponty studies.

²I have dealt with this more fully in: James M. Edie, *Speaking and Meaning*, Indiana University Press, 1976, Chapter III.

³James M. Edie, "Foreword," Maurice Merleau-Ponty, *Consciousness and The Acquisition of Language*, tr. Hugh J. Silverman, Northwestern University Press, 1973, pp. xix-xx.

⁴Claude Lefort, "Editor's Preface," Maurice Merleau-Ponty, *The Prose of the World*, tr. John O'Neill, Northwestern University Press, 1973, pp. pp. xv ff.

⁵Maurice Merleau-Ponty, *Signs*, tr. Richard C. McCleary, Northwestern University Press, 1964, p. 117.

⁶Maurice Merleau-Ponty, *Themes from the Lectures at the Collège de France*, tr. John O'Neill, Northwestern University Press, 1970, pp. 19-20.

⁷See "Foreword," *Consciousness and the Acquisition of Language, op. cit.*, pp. xxvii-xxix.

⁸*Consciousness and the Acquisition of Language, op. cit.*, p. 93.

⁹*Ibid.*, p. 97.

¹⁰*Ibid.*, p. 99.

¹¹*Ibid.*, p. 93.

¹²Maurice Merleau-Ponty, "Phenomenology and the Sciences of Man," *The Primacy of Perception*, ed. James M. Edie, Northwestern University Press, 1964, pp. 81-82.

¹³*Ibid.*, p. 81.

¹⁴*Ibid.*

¹⁵*Ibid.*, p. 84.

¹⁶Maurice Merleau-Ponty, *In Praise of Philosophy*, tr. James M. Edie and John Wild, Northwestern University Press, 1963, p 56, emphasis mine.

¹⁷*Ibid.*, pp. 54-55.

¹⁸James M. Edie, "Phenomenology in the United States (1974)," *Journal of the British Society for Phenomenology*, 1974, pp. 206 ff. In this article I think I demonstrate the importance of Gurwitsch for Merleau-Ponty and provide the essential, though perhaps not the exhaustive, bibliographical information relevant to their collaboration in the years 1933-1940. The article by Gurwitsch, "Quelques aspects et quelques développements de la psychologie de la forme," *Journal de psychologie normale et pathologique*, 1936, pp. 413-470, was one on which Merleau-Ponty is cited as a collaborator; it is also one which provided the French philosophical world of that time with the most extensive bibliography on Gestalt theory which had been published up to that time. This bibliography is very similar to that in Merleau-Ponty's *Structure of Behavior*.

¹⁹*Consciousness and the Acquisition of Language, op. cit.*, p. 100.

²⁰Raymond Boudon, *A quoi sert la notion de "structure"?* Paris, 1968, p. 42, and *passim*.

²¹James M. Edie, *Speaking and Meaning, op. cit.*, pp. 75 ff.

²²Maurice Merleau-Ponty, *Sense and Non-Sense* tr. Dreyfus, Northwestern University Press, 1964, p. 63.

²³Maurice Merleau-Ponty, "An Unpublished Text," *Primacy of Perception, op. cit.*, pp. 3-11. This "Prospectus" of Merleau-Ponty's work, written by himself, and carefully interpreted by Claude Lefort in the "Editor's Preface" to *The Prose of the World*, was Merleau-Ponty's own assessment of his past achievements and his plans for future work at the time he presented himself as a candidate for a chair at the Collège de France.

²⁴The principal flaw of a recent study (Samuel B. Mallin, *Merleau-Ponty's*

Philosophy, Yale University Press, 1979) is that it bases itself on "Merleau-Ponty's full-length works, the *Phenomenology of Perception* and *The Visible and the Invisible*" (p. 4). Whatever the justification for leaving out Merleau-Ponty's other books, there is no justification *at all* for treating *The Visible and the Invisible* as a completed work in any sense. As a work of interpretation this book (by Mullin) attempts to explain *the clear* by *the obscure*.

[25]This point has been made very cogently, with complete historical documentation, by George L. Kline, "The Existentialist Rediscovery of Hegel and Marx," *Phenomenology and Existentialism*, eds. Lee and Mandelbaum, Johns Hopkins University Press, 1967, pp. 113 ff.

[26]Though the opposite principle of interpretation, in the case of Merleau-Ponty, might bear fruit. He himself always interpreted his newest ideas in terms of earlier periods. Thus he re-interprets his dialectical interpretation of phenomenology in terms of Gestalt theory, and his structuralism in terms of both Gestaltism and dialectics. He could not, of course, interpret his unfinished last work in terms of the earlier except in the most incohate manner since he died before completing it. But perhaps his commentators should ponder his own attitude towards his development rather than imposing the criterion: the last is best.

[27]Here, in full justice to Merleau-Ponty, it is necessary to remark that he never fell into the excesses of *Derridian* post-structuralism (or deconstructionism) which holds that all "texts" are self-referential. Thus the "post-structuralism" (if I can call it that for want of a better term) of *The Visible and the Invisible* is an entirely different matter from what the Derridians have come to. With his fine sensitivity to the complexities of language in its relation to experience Merleau-Ponty writes, thus, in a typical passage: "It is the error the semantic philosophies to close up language as if it spoke only of itself: *language lives only from silence*; everything we cast to the others has germinated in this great mute land which we never leave. But, because he has experienced within himself the need to speak . . . the Philosopher knows better than anyone . . . that the vision itself, the thought itself, are, as has been said [by Lacan] 'structured like language' " *The Visible and the Invisible*, p. 126, emphasis mine. There is a "post-structuralism" about Merleau-Ponty's final thought, but it needs to be given a nuanced interpretation which would eschew equating it with what otherwise goes by that name. I would here like to express my debt to Professor Dorothy Leland who read her comments and critical remarks on this paper at the meeting of the American Philosophical Association in San Francisco in March, 1980. I have greatly profited from her suggestions, on this and other points.

[28]*The Visible and the Invisible, op. cit.*, p. 65.

[29]See, for instance, the papers in *Deconstruction and Criticism*, Bloom, de Man, Derrida, Hartman, Miller, New York, 1979 *passim*. Since most of the persons who treat of dialectical logic in this manner are not, strictly speaking, philosophers but literary critics, and since they write with a special hermetic style better understood by baptized initiates than those who argue openly in the forum, it is not always clear exactly what they are affirming with respect to deconstructionist methodology. It was, therefore, a great pleasure for the present author to be able to ask, at the recent meeting of the International Association for Philosophy and Literature, held in Orono, Maine, in May, 1980, two "deconstructionists," namely professors Michael Murray and Rodolphe Gaschè, at separate meetings, the question of whether or not their conception of dialectics and their conception of their method required the renunciation of the principles of non-contradiction and of identity as these are defined and understood in formal logic. Both men answered with straightforward, honest, one-word responses: "Yes."

[30]*The Visible and the Invisible, op. cit.*, p. 142.

[31]*Ibid.*, p. 123.

[32]Albert Rabil, *Merleau-Ponty, Existentialist of the Social World*, Columbia University Press, 1967, pp. 144 ff.

[33]*The Prose of the World, op. cit.*, pp. 38 ff., 115 ff., and Edie, *Speaking and Meaning. op. cit.*, pp. 112 ff.

[34]Cf. the forthcoming study by Errol Harris, *Formal and Dialectical Logic*. Harris gives careful, detailed, rigorous attention first, to the metaphysical presuppositions of formal logic *as such*, then to the transcendental presuppositions of formal logic, and, finally, to the "formal" presuppositions of dialectical logic.

Merleau-Ponty. From Dialectic to Hyperdialectic[1]

JACQUES TAMINIAUX
Université de Louvain-la-Neuve

In the book left unfinished at his death, Merleau-Ponty wrote; "The bad dialectic begins almost with the dialectic, and there is no dialectic but that which criticizes itself and surpasses itself as a separate statement; the only good dialectic is the hyperdialectic."[2]

What about this good dialectic which his last writing sought to practice? Rather than address this question directly, I would like to prepare for it instead by inquiring into the status of dialectic in Merleau-Ponty's itinerary. Since the final work strives to demarcate good and bad dialectic from one another, I would like to ask about this demarcation and its possible avatars in the earlier works. Supposing that such a demarcation indeed figures there, in what sense can Merleau-Ponty lay claim to a 'dialectical thinking,' why does he see it as entitled to validity, and for what fault, if any, does he criticize it?

I. If we address such a question to the first two books, *The Structure of Behavior*[3] and the *Phenomenology of Perception*,[4] we quickly realize that it is premature. The question supposes, in effect, that in these books there is a genuine confrontation with dialectical thinking; an effort to partition what is essential to it from what is merely accident, or from what denatures it. But such a confrontation does not take place. Both books struggle at length with Cartesianism, empiricism, realism, criticism, and reflexive thinking; the second of the two inaugurates a confrontation with the phenomenology of Husserl, while neither explicitly confronts dialectical thinking. It would be wrong to conclude that dialectical thinking is nowhere to be encountered; on the contrary, it is greeted positively, though in an allusive manner, as a mode of intelligibility suited to the phenomenal field to which these works are trying to gain access.

Take, for instance, *The Structure of Behavior*. Recall the purpose of this work. It aims to understand afresh the relations between consciousness and nature by surpassing the two solutions applied to this problem by prevailing thought: the critical solution, which consists in stripping nature of all substantiality by making it into an ensemble of functional relationships constituted by consciousness; and the realist solution, which consists in making of nature a real substance, a *res* divisible into parts mutually bound by causal relationships, and in situating consciousness with respect to this *res*, whether by integrating it therein, or by juxtaposing it alongside as a specific *res*. Properly speaking, however, it is not a matter of a joint critique of the two solutions. The critique is first aimed at realist and causal thinking, showing that it does violence to the phenomena of which it treats; and only subsequently, after having withdrawn the phenomena from this violence, does the critique show the difficulty of a pure and simple return to the classical transcendental perspective of Kantian inspiration. In other words, although there is indeed an actual refutation of realism, there is only a correction of criticism. What on the one hand founds the refutations, and on the other summons the correction, is the direct elucidation of what Watson had called "behavior"; something he had rightly intuited as the confrontation between man or any organism and a world, but wrongly interpreted within the framework of realist and causal thought. Pursuing the fundamentally sound intuition of Watson, but denying the indigent philosophy within which he had inscribed it, Merleau-Ponty applies himself to procuring an adequate philosophical status for this new notion of behavior, and it is here that he welcomes dialectical thinking positively for the first time. In a long footnote appended to the Introduction of the book—drafted while it was already at the printers—Merleau-Ponty manifestly takes stock of the position he had won: "In our opinion (. . .), when Watson spoke of behavior he had in mind what others have called *existence*; but the new notion could receive its philosophical status only if causal or mechanical thinking were abandoned for dialectical thinking" (SB 226, n3). This sentence, one might say, sketches out the style and limits of Merleau-Ponty's initial relationship with dialectical thinking. On the one hand, it asserts that the meaning and mode of being of behavior, however rudimentarily examined, needs to be thought

dialectically—and that mechanical and causal thinking are utterly un-
suited to this task. On the other hand and reciprocally, it supposes
that Merleau-Ponty uses dialectical thinking only in order to think the
meaning of behavior. In other words, behavior understood as confrontation with the world is the norm and measure of
Merleau-Ponty's recourse to dialectical thinking. This becomes even
more evident when we refer to those analyses in the body of the text
which introduce the epithet 'dialectical' or the syntagme 'dialectical
thinking.' These terms are introduced at the end of a long critique,
first of the notion of reflex behavior, then of realist explanations of
so-called 'higher forms of behavior.' Against the classical definition
of reflex, Merleau-Ponty invokes several physiological and
psychological works whose contribution, in his eyes, seems to consist
in the substitution of the notion of 'structure' or 'form' in place of the
classical notion of the 'elemental unit.' The notion of form implies not
only the predominance of ensembles over atomic units, but also a
causal relation between the organism and its milieu that is not linear
but 'circular.' This circularity is furthermore indissociable from a
'signification'; that is, it submits to the exigencies of maintaining an
optimal equilibrium between the organism and its milieu, as well as of
maintaining its own internal equilibrium.

Against the realist, causal, and atomistic pursuit of 'higher
behaviors,' or behaviors which testify to an aptitude for acquiring new
reactions, Merleau-Ponty advances numerous observations along
similar lines which call upon us to envision learning as a process of
structuration which establishes an internal relation between the means
and the end, as well as a signifying relation between the situation and
the response of the living organism. This priority of structure bids us
to surpass the classical distinction between elementary and complex
conducts in favor of a hierarchy of behaviors according to the type of
structure they embody—syncretic, amovable, or symbolic—and above
all to surpass the alternative of *res* and *cogitatio*. To acknowledge that
behavior is a form or structure is to acknowledge that it is not a *res*,
since it does not disperse *partes extra partes*; also that it is not a
cogitatio, since what it expresses does not betray "a being whose
whole essence is to know," but only "a certain manner of treating the
world" (SB 125). Such is precisely the mode of being Merleau-Ponty
qualifies as 'dialectical.' He invokes this term to designate while also
to embrace the diverse aspects of the notion of Gestalt or structure.

The first of these aspects is 'circularity.' The relations between the
individual organism and his milieu are said to be 'dialectical' because
"the organism itself measures the action of things upon it and itself

delimits its milieu by a circular process'' (SB 148).

The second is 'signifying totalization.' Because the particularities of an organism and its mode of action symbolize each other, and because its unity is a unity of signification, the organism is said to exhibit a 'vital dialectic' (SB 156). In this context Merleau-Ponty invokes a quote from Hegel's Jena *Logic*: "The mind of nature is a hidden mind . . . it is mind in itself, but not for itself" (SB 161), and he goes to the point of suggesting that to philosophize according to the Gestalt is—contrary to the attempts of Gestalt Theory to obliterate the meaning of its discoveries by drawing philosophical conclusions which only restore the realism of causal thinking—to acknowledge that the true Gestalt is close to the Gestalt in the Hegelian sense; namely, he says, the "concept before it has become consciousness of self" (SB 210). Hegel is again invoked in the discussion of the philosophical status of properly human—or 'symbolic'—structures. The relation of man to his world is not reducible to the relation 'vital situation-instinctive reaction.' Instead it exhibits a specific dialectic owing its originality to another binary relation, 'perceived situation-work,' this last term understood in the Hegelian sense as designating "the ensemble of activities by which man transforms physical and living nature" (SB 162). The Hegelian negativity and mediation are certainly implicit here, since Merleau-Ponty later adds that "the meaning of human work" is "the taking possession of an indefinite space and time," and that it reveals not only "the capacity of orienting oneself in relation to the possible, to the mediate," but also "the capacity of rejecting the given milieu and of searching for equilibrium beyond any milieu" (SB 175-6, 245 n97).

There remains another properly dialectical aspect of the notion of Gestalt. The mind of nature, wrote Hegel, "is only mind for the mind which knows it." In reality then, Merleau-Ponty adds while commenting on the stages of his own description, "we have already introduced consciousness and what we have designated under the name of life was already consciousness of life" (SB 161-2). That life is already consciousness of life means here that, since life offers itself in all respects as a structure or a form, and since form ultimately belongs to the perceptive order, *there is no form except for a perceptive consciousness*. The human order of consciousness is thus the universal condition of possibility and the ultimate presupposition, and the movement of Merleau-Ponty's thought here is well within the sphere of transcendental thinking inaugurated by Kant. With one major corrective, however. Precisely because the consciousness everywhere presupposed is perceptive, it can no longer be envisioned as an 'I think' which accompanies all of my representations, or as an epistemological subject whose objective correlate is a pure signification. If the Gestalt must be envisioned as "the concept before it has become consciousness of self," what is profound here is not the idea of signification, but that of 'structure,' or "the joining of an idea and an existence which are indiscernible, the contingent arrangement by which materials begin to have meaning in our presence, intelligibility in the nascent state" (SB 206-7). Correlatively, the perceiving consciousness presupposed by the structures itself has a mode of existence both contingent and laden with a structure. And here a final properly dialectical implication of the notion of Gestalt appears. Just as there is a circularity between the organism and its milieu, so there is also a circularity between existence and consciousness. Citing Hegel anew, Merleau-Ponty writes; "For life, as for the mind, there is no past which is absolutely past; 'the moments which the mind seems to have behind it are also borne in its present depths' " (SB 207). This signifies that the supposed purity of the epistemological subject is bound to conditions of existence which indeed are "indiscernible in the whole with which they collaborate," but are such that "the essence of the whole cannot be concretely conceptualized without them and without its constitutive history." In other words, the emergence of the epistemological subject is to be understood as "the institution of a new dialectic . . . the establishment of a new constitutive layer which eliminates the preceding one as isolated moment, but conserves and integrates it" (SB 208).

Taken as a whole, the investigation conducted by Merleau-Ponty in *The Structure of Behavior* qualifies itself as a dialectical one for two major reasons. First, because of its phenomenal content. The mode of manifestation of behavior envisioned from the lowest level upwards and, as Merleau-Ponty says, from the point of view of the 'outside spectator' exhibits dialectical traits: 'circularity' between the living organism and its milieu; 'signifying totalization' in the sense of a reciprocal symbolization of being and action, of partial activities and global conduct; and finally 'negativity' in the specifically human symbolic comportments. As these three characteristics are those of Gestalten, one might say that the very phenomenality of Gestalt is dialectical. But besides the descriptive content of the Gestalt the investigation also concerns the transcendental conditions of possibility of the Gestalt. Just as life, according to Hegel, refers back to consciousness of life, so the Gestalt refers back to consciousness of Gestalt. At this juncture the investigation qualifies itself as dialectical for a second reason, pertaining to this transcendental aspect. The

Gestalt presupposes a perceiving consciousness as its transcendental condition. But perceiving consciousness, in turn, is a structure. This means that it is itself affected by all the traits of what it renders possible; that the negativity permeating it, as well as its proper mode of signification, never permit it to detach itself from a circular confrontation with a world; and that the *Aufhebung* that it effects remains affected by what is surpassed.

The cogency of the Introduction footnote is now clear: behavior or Gestalt as confrontation with the world is indeed, and in every respect, the norm of Merleau-Ponty's recourse to dialectical thinking.

II. But this same note asserts that behavior thus understood is what others have called 'existence.' We are therefore led to the *Phenomenology of Perception*, since this second book deems itself entirely existential philosophy. Here an attentive study of the text will show that it is this time existence which is taken as the norm of the recourse to dialectical thinking. In this perspective, for instance, the Idea in the Hegelian sense will be said to be that formula "which sums up some unique manner of behavior towards others, towards Nature, time, and death: a certain way of patterning the world" (PP xviii), or which constitutes a unique core of existential signification at the intersection of a plurality of perspectives. But inversely, as any core of existential signification is inseparable from a plurality of perspectives, immeshing my past into my present, the other into myself, and myself into him, Merleau-Ponty will say that meaning can in no event "be set in a realm apart, transposed into absolute spirit" (PP xix-xx). Although allusions to dialectical thinking are overall less numerous in the *Phenomenology of Perception* than in *The Structure of Behavior*, these two works taken together sketch out the characteristic style of Merleau-Ponty's first encounter with dialectical thinking. Dialectical thinking is not thematized as such, but hailed in passing insofar as Merleau-Ponty believes an existential tenor can be recognized in it, and cast aside insofar as it is unfaithful to the condition of Being-in-the-world.

This is also the style which predominates in those writings of the same period in which, on the basis of his first two books, Merleau-Ponty explicitly considers the writings of Hegel and Marx. It is striking to verify just how little these writings bother to translate themselves into the text of Hegel or Marx, and how zealously, instead, they scurry to translate these texts into the terms of *The Structure of Behavior* or the *Phenomenology of Perception*.

Consider the article in *Sense and Non-Sense*[5] entitled, "Hegel's Existentialism.'' Here Merleau-Ponty treats the *Phenomenology of Spirit*. ''But if the Hegel of 1827 may be criticized for his idealism,'' he writes, ''the same cannot be said of the Hegel of 1807,'' adding that it is ''certain'' that ''the *Phenomenology of Spirit* does not try to fit all history into a framework of pre-established logic'' (SN 64). It would be vain, I think, to try to justify this proposition advanced by Merleau-Ponty by appealing to Hegel himself, for three reasons. First of all, any allegation of a supposed opposition between the Hegel of 1807 and of 1827 disregards the fact that the architectonic and the conceptual apparatus of the so-called mature system were both established at the time of the Jena writings. Furthermore, this thesis silently overlooks Hegel's stated project of this period: the realization of an absolute idealism. Finally, it conflicts with the most recent results of the *Hegelforschung*, which tend to show that a preestablished logic does indeed found the articulation of the *Phenomenology of Spirit*. But if Merleau-Ponty's proposition cannot be justified by appealing to Hegel's writings, it may be justified—in effect—by appealing to those of Merleau-Ponty. When Merleau-Ponty writes, ''Hegel's thought is existentialist in that it views man not as being from the start a consciousness in full possession of its own clear thoughts, but as a life which is its own responsibility and which tries to understand itself,'' and when he adds that the Hegelian oeuvre describes ''man's efforts to reappropriate himself'' (SN 65), these remarks only make sense when they are understood, not in terms of the Hegelian relation between natural consciousness and absolute knowledge, but against the background of Merleau-Ponty's conception of the relation between the unreflective and reflection. Furthermore, the first relation must be merged into the second and displaced onto the humanist terrain of the existential project, thereby cutting it off at the same stroke from the Hegelian wellspring; namely, the presuppositions of the Absolute which, from the outset, ''is and wants to be alongside us.'' The same could be said of the other themes which Merleau-Ponty culls from the *Phenomenology of Spirit*. Anxiety, consciousness of death, and the struggle between consciousnesses are not introduced for the purpose of learning what they signify in Hegel, but as pretexts to reaffirm that consciousness is not a *res*, and that the mode of being human is an ambiguous one because life and death, solitude and communication never cease to intermingle in it.

What about the essays relating to the thought of Marx? Here the text itself seems to have been taken into consideration—which was scarcely true in the case of Hegel. Still, Marx's tests meet a similar encroachment as that which governed the reading of Hegel. The principle of this reading is announced by Merleau-Ponty himself: "Concrete thinking, which Marx calls 'critique' to distinguish it from speculative philosophy, is what others propound under the name 'existential philosophy' " (SN 133). If the Marxist critique—namely, that critico-praxis which Marx, during the years 1843-4, opposed simultaneously to a praxis without philosophical horizon and to a critique which never left the ground of self-consciousness—if this critique is indeed what others propound under the name 'existential philosophy,' then it cannot be Merleau-Ponty's intention to interrogate its Hegelian filia-tion, nor even to inquire into the ontological principles which unify the traits of this filiation in the text of Marx, still less to search for what is unthought in it, but rather to transpose this critique into the terms and foundations of existential philosophy. Some examples will suffice to make this transposition manifest. When Marx writes in the *Contribution to the Critique of Hegel's "Philosophy of Right,"* "You cannot overcome philosophy without realizing it," in context this signifies that the absolute identity of subject and object is going to find the means of 'becoming world' in the proletariat. Merleau-Ponty translates this as follows: "The *cogito* is false only in that it removes itself and shatters our inherence in the world. The only way to over-come it is to realize it, that is, to show that it is eminently contained in interpersonal relations" (SN 133). As he makes explicit further on, this means that "the human subject thinks in terms of his situation," that he finds himself "in the midst of other consciousnesses which likewise have a situation;" in short, that subjectivity is intersubjectivi-ty (SN 133-4).

Similarly, when Marx writes in the *Manuscripts of 1844* that "naturalism or realized humanism differ from idealism as much as from materialism and is at the same time the truth uniting both," Merleau-Ponty hastens to decipher it, without troubling to inquire in-to the Feuerbachian soil from which such formulae grow, in the light of his own project of a conjoint surpassing of realism and intellec-tualism, to such an extent that it signifies for him that man is neither pure consciousness nor inert thing, but relation to a world; that is, an engagement which has "an exterior aspect, an outside . . . which is 'objective' at the same time as 'subjective' " (SN 130).

Finally, when Marx writes that "for man the root is man himself," or that "he produces himself" and is himself his own origin, everything happens as if Merleau-Ponty found in these sentences an equivalent of the Heideggerian distinction between *Vorhandenheit* and *Da-Sein*, since he takes them as signifying that man "not only is, but exists," without so much as suspecting that at virtually the same time Heidegger was situating the Marxist self-production at the anti-podes of the ek-static mode of being of Dasein. One may argue that these writings on Marx are topical, indissociable from the political atmosphere in which the French intelligensia basked during the early post-war period, and that after all the intent of these texts is peda-gogical—to point out to those who reject existential philosophy in the name of Marx what in his writings could be said to sanction it. Such indeed seems to be the aim of these texts; it is centripetal and without being arbitrary one may transpose to the relationship which Merleau-Ponty's texts form with Marx what he told us of Marx's relationship with phenomenology: "A purely philological examination of the texts in question would yield nothing; we find in texts only what we put into them, and if ever any kind of history has suggested the interpretations which should be put on it, it is the history of philosophy. We shall find in ourselves, and nowhere else, the unity and true meaning of phenomenology" (PP viii). Just as there is what he calls "a phenomenology for ourselves," which recognizes what it had been waiting for, so there is also a "Marxism for ourselves."

But what is this "Marxism for ourselves"? And, in jeopardy of hav-ing to admit that Merleau-Ponty's relation to the history of thought is a pure projection, what are the properly philosophical principles, common to both Marx and Merleau-Ponty, which found this retrieve or reappropriation? We shall doubtless have the best chance of find-ing the elements of a response to this question by turning to his most elaborate essay on Marxism, *Humanism and Terror*. This effort re-quires, in my opinion, that we go beyond the topical character of the essay to try to disengage the properly philosophical theses. The pretext for the book was Arthur Koestler's romantic interpretation of the Moscow trials in *Darkness at Noon*. This interpretation, Merleau-Ponty asserts, demonstrates that Koestler is not a Marxist. This does not prevent it from posing an acute problem, however; that of effec-tive communism. I shall not broach this second problem, but only the first: that of Marxist thinking.

Merleau-Ponty finds the proof that Koestler is not a Marxist in the alternatives governing his manner of thinking; efficacy and morality, historical determinism and Kantian imperative, Commissar and Yogi, in short subjective and objective. But it is the privilege of Marxism to have surpassed these alternatives. Koestler's novel describes characters who "believe it is necessary to choose between the interior and the exterior," who decide that consciousness is nothing, who sub-mit themselves to a scientific and mechanistic view of the political state that will ultimately crush them, and who adhere to a 'technical logic' which transforms everything into inert objects. Marx, according to Merleau-Ponty, recognizes in history, however, a "living logic . . . which expresses itself indivisibly by objective necessities and by the spontaneous movement of the masses" (HT 15), with the result that, instead of absolutizing history as a grand machinery whose truth yields itself to the impersonal inquiry of science, he makes it rest upon the blending of human perspectives. For Marx, writes Merleau-Ponty, "interhuman praxis is the absolute" (HT 18).

Here the first philosophical principle founding Merleau-Ponty's retrieve of the teaching of Marx reveals itself; the 'absoluteness of praxis.' He expresses it in these terms: "The only history of which we may speak is that whose image and future we construct, by means of interpretations which are simultaneously methodical and creative" (HT 20). This history is dialectical inasmuch as it returns against itself, and this, "in the final analysis, because men enter into collision with structures which alienate them, because the economic subject is a human subject" (HT 23). To the extent that it accomplishes an interchange of subjective and objective, Marx's conception of history escapes the alternative of scientism and nominalism, since it surpasses the former by integrating the lived, and the latter by practically realizing the abstract imperatives of the ethics of pure intentions. A second principle is derived from the absoluteness of praxis; the 'radical contingency of the liberal pact' which proclaims the universality of the rights of man. This pact does not express the properties of human nature. It is but a historical product, and the universality it appeals to is but a class reason, while the spontaneous practice of the proletariat, given the universality of the concrete situation of oppression that it sustains, is always in the process of realizing a no longer merely formal but effective universality. Moreover, this contingency of liberalism implies an unacknowledged violence which, because it is deliberately overlooked, can only perpetuate itself. Revolutionary violence, on the other hand, admits itself as such, being the willful negation of the established violence, thus the negation of the negation.

But a third principle, of 'historical responsibility,' is also derived from the absoluteness of praxis and surpasses, like the second principle, the classical doublets intention and act, and subjective and objective, adhered to by liberal thinking. Honesty of intention does not prohibit the historical act from being guilty if it happens that its objective consequences entail a weakening of the chances of the concrete realization of the universal. It is precisely because history is not inscribed in things, but is relatively unforseeable and thus created and decided in risk, that its course in the wake of a decision first brings this decision into the tribunal's jurisdiction only *a posteriori*. This contingency condemns the political man to being an 'unhappy consciousness,' and condemns the revolutionary to being a 'tragic hero,' since in the name of the revolution the ruling power imputes to him as a crime an opposing position which he had believed favorable to the revolution, while at the same time it is impossible for him to associate himself fully with the forces crushing him, since insofar as the revolution is inachieved it is still undecided who has the better deciphered history, the ruling power or himself. Merleau-Ponty found in these principles the secret of Bukharin's confession during the Moscow trials, and also rested upon them the idea that there is no absolute difference between Lenin, Stalin, and Trotsky, for all three acknowledge contingency and the open exercise of terror as a violence that is not gratuitous but oriented towards a human future.

III. The question here is not to discover whether this interpretation of the immediate historical situation stands up to scrutiny, but to pursue further the investigation of the philosophical principles which articulate Merleau-Ponty's 'Marxism for ourselves.' When he says that praxis is the absolute, this signifies on the one hand that, just as there is no nature in itself, so there is no history in itself, and on the other that the pure for-itself is an abstraction, an unreality. In no longer negative but positive terms, this means that consciousness exists only as incarnated and situated, or, as he says, that consciousnesses "intermingle with the situation assumed by themselves, and could not complain if one confused them with it and if one neglected the so-called incorruptible innocence of conscience" (HT 109). This thesis is dialectical in the sense that it assumes the Hegelian critique of the 'beautiful soul' and the general tenor of Kantian morality; also in the sense that in its implications it rejoins the Hegelian analyses of the struggle of self-consciousnesses and of the 'unhappy consciousness.' They rejoin the Hegelian analysis of self-consciousness, for to say that consciousness intermingles with the situation it assumes is also to say that it enters necessarily into a struggle with others, that it cannot abstract itself from the perspective which others have on it, and that consciousness never ceases to make use of them and to be what it does unto them—and is therefore originally inscribed in violence.

The implications of the absoluteness of praxis also rejoin the Hegelian analysis of the 'unhappy consciousness.' By virtue of its situation and of the violence of intersubjectivity, consciousness fells the lack of coincidence between what it is and what it thinks, between what it wills and what it does, as a permanent drama.

But Merleau-Ponty's position in *Humanism and Terror* is yet dialectical for another reason. For Hegel the figures of the struggle and of the 'unhappy consciousness' are joined by virtue of being moments in the perspective of an identity between being and thought. Strangely enough, we do not find it otherwise for Merleau-Ponty. Just as tragedy as Hegel understood it—the collision of a knowing and a non-knowing—far from being irremediable, is only the promise of a higher synthesis, likewise the tragedy of the revolutionary condition, as described by Merleau-Ponty, is inscribed within the perspective of its abolition. A careful reading of the text will show that, however carefully he tries to repair the paradoxes of acting, embodied intersubjectivity, an interrogation of the revolutionary *telos* as such never materializes. This is clearly evident in those analyses where he subscribes to the Marxist theory of the proletariat. "The theory of the proletariat is not an annex nor an appendix in Marxism," he writes. "It is truly the center of the doctrine, for it is in proletarian existence that abstract conceptions become life and that life makes itself consciousness . . . The theory of the proletariat absolutely distinguishes a Marxist politics from all other authoritarian politics, and makes the formal analogies which are often pointed out between them utterly superficial" (HT 113). What are the distinctive features of the Marxist concept of the proletariat? Marx thinks of the proletariat as a *de facto* universal, Merleau-Ponty claims; a universal which is not merely conceived but lived. Its condition—thus, its socio-economic condition—is such that in it the reign of particularities is transcended: "It is the universality which it thinks," and it thinks the universality which it is. It is the sole authentic intersubjectivity because in its alone "the separation and the union of individuals are simultaneously lived" and because "it alone is in a universal situation" (HT 116). The violence or terror assumed but not created by Marxism is transcended through the proletariat. The alternatives of real and ideal, Machiavelli and Kant, means and ends, fact and value, power and ethics, are also transcended therein. That he assumes this synthetic concept of the proletariat—"the identity of the subjective and the objective" (HT 137)—is demonstrated by his translation of it into the language of intersubjectivity, and especially by the application he makes of one of his dearest notions, the Gestalt, to the Marxist concept of history as the happening of the universal in the proletariat.

> To be Marxist is to think that the economic questions and the cultural or human questions are a single question, and that the proletariat such as history has made it contains the solution to this unique problem. To speak a modern

language, it is to think that history is a *Gestalt*, in the sense
that German authors give this word, a total process of
movement towards a state of equilibrium, the classless
society, which could not be attained without effort and
without human action, but which indicates itself in the present crises as a resolution of these crises, as the power of
man over nature and reconciliation of man with man (HT
130).

It might be objected that Merleau-Ponty's analyses of the immediate historical situation questions this concept. But upon closer examination it is not this concept which Merleau-Ponty criticizes, but
only certain concrete forms in which it has been realized—Stalinist
authoritarianism and a general recession of internationalism and of
the initiative of the masses, for instance. In other words, the actual
tenor of the concept of the proletariat in the Marxist sense is not interrogated as such. After checking off all those factors contradicting the
realization of those things augured and willed by Marxism, Merleau-
Ponty asks himself the following question: "But why grant a respite to
this philosophy? It has not succeeded in becoming reality; it is a
utopia." To which he replies: "Considered closely, Marxism is not
just any hypothesis which can be replaced tomorrow by some other. It
is the simple statement of those conditions without which there would
neither be any humanism, in the sense of a reciprocal relation between
men, nor any rationality in history; it is *the* philosophy of history, and
to give it up completely would be to strike out historical reason" (HT
156). The proletarian Gestalt is not one form among others; it is *the*
'good form' of history, without which history would be merely a col-
lection of insignificant facts.

It is evident that a sizeable equivocation in Merleau-Ponty's texts is
generated by this unquestioned retrieve of the synthetic concept of the
proletariat as the realizing agent of authentic intersubjectivity and of
the meaning of history; an equivocation affecting, most immediately,
the internal economy of his thought. It is one thing to say that intersubjectivity is paradoxical and ambiguous, that there is a drama of
Being-with-others, that the moment there is another's perspective on
me and of me on him there is violence, that embodiment is
simultaneously the condition and limit of liberty, that the sense which
it inaugurates is always accompanied by a non-sense—and quite
another to say that authentic intersubjectivity is the concrete realization of a universal which transcends all particularity, which identifies
the subjective and the objective, and which inaugurates an equilibrium
such that only then and through it does history finally become reason.

This equivocation concerns the very concept of dialectic itself, and affects the very manner in which it is understood by Merleau-Ponty. In the first instance the dialectic is not synthesis but persistent interchange of contraries—hence ambiguity—while in the second it is truly identity—hence effacement of ambiguity. But if this equivocation is to be possible; if the same concepts, for instance that of intersubjectivity, could be understood on some occasions as ambiguous and on others as synthetic, then we must ask whether it is not generalized, whether this equivocation does not affect each and every one of these concepts. We have seen that when Merleau-Ponty established his initial relation to dialectical thinking, it was behavior as confrontation with a world, or again as existence, which functioned as the norm and privileged domain of dialectic. We also encountered this same norm and privileged domain in those writings on Marx and Hegel contemporary with the *Phenomenology of Perception*, and once again in *Humanism and Terror*. Let us recall the famous sentence from the Conclusion to this latter book: "There is as much existentialism in the 'Stenographic Transcript' of the Moscow trials as in all the works of Heidegger" (HT 187). This sentence is, as it were, the symptomatic distillation of an entire way of thinking which appears strange and even shallow to us today, consisting of a generalized practice of rapprochement and encroachment, to which the following phrases, selected almost at random, testify: "the whole of *Sein und Zeit* springs from an indication by Husserl" (PP vii); "the introduction of the notion of the *human object*, which phenomenology has taken up and developed, was reserved for Marx" (SN 131); and finally, "the 'metaphysical' content of Marxism, in the Heideggerian sense, consists of men in the process of taking nature (to which they were at first subordinate) upon themselves, of rupturing the given structures of society, and of acceding through praxis to the 'reign of liberty,' or, as Hegel said, to 'absolute history' " (SN 127-8). The unsuitability of this practice is that it is only possible by detaching those themes allowing the rapprochements effected from the principles grounding them in the original text—for instance, from Hegel's "will of the *Absolute* to be from the start alongside us," or from Heidegger's *Seinsfrage*. But my aim is less to discover the unsuitability of this practice than to discover what, in the final analysis, founds these rapprochements and encroachments. More precisely, since our concern is dialectic and since Marx played a dominant role in Merleau-Ponty's retrieve of dialectical thinking, to discover what founds the superimposition of Merleau-Ponty's text on that of Marx. We have seen that it is ultimately behavior as Being-in-the-world, or again as existence, that functions as the privileged location of the dialectic. Despite Merleau-Ponty's cavalier assertion to the effect that we only find in the history of philosophy what we await there, something in the text of Marx has to solicit such superimposition, or else we have to admit that this retrieve is a purely arbitrary projection. This something Merleau-Ponty himself puts into relief in the exergue to his article on "Marxism and Philosophy," a quotation from the *Contribution to the Critique of Hegel's Philosophy of Right*: "To be radical is to grasp things by the root. But for man, the root is man himself." For Marx this means that man as self-productivity has the status of the ultimate ontological principle, and that Merleau-Ponty recognizes himself in it signifies that he indeed has understood self-production as Being-in-the-world.

Here we reach the essential moment of the inquiry. It seems to me beyond doubt that the Marxist self-production is decidedly inscribed within the modern heritage of Cartesian subjectivity, absolutized by Hegel. The Marxist project can be conceived as the realization of the Hegelian speculative equation: absolute certitude of Self or the Same in its Other, or of Substance in the Subject. Themes such as the identity of accomplished humanism and accomplished naturalism spoken of in the *Manuscripts of 1844*, history as man's production by man, and praxis as the path of man's self-recognition in nature and of man in other men, are all decipherable as realizations of Hegelian speculation, as offspring of the Cartesian *cogito*. Merleau-Ponty began by superimposing the existentialist theme of the project over the Marxist theme of praxis. This implies, if not the resolute adoption, at least the unquestioned retrieve of that first principle of modern thought, subjectivity. And if Merleau-Ponty objects to the Cartesian *res* from the start, it is *de facto* not for the purpose of objecting to the *cogito* as such, but rather of correcting it. Perception corrects but by no means abolishes the primacy of subjectivity. Let us recall that famous text where Merleau-Ponty objects to the Cartesian *realitas*, and erects the mode of being of perception upon the Ego: "I am the absolute source . . . for I alone bring into being for myself (and therefore into being in the only sense that the word can have for me) the tradition which I elect to carry on, or the horizon whose distance from me would be abolished . . .if I were not there to scan it with my gaze" (PP ix). In its ontological import Being as Being-for-me is the very definition of the *cogito*, of *Bewusstsein*. To be in-the-world does not mean for Merleau-Ponty to be ek-statically open to Being which withdraws and conceals itself; it means to be as an Ego for a Being which is essentially for me. This is precisely the dialectical formula of the Hegelian speculative circle, of which existentialism is but one version. Perhaps this reveals the incentive for the tenacity with which Merleau-Ponty everywhere sets himself to refuting objectivist thinking and conditioning by external causation. If I produce myself, my outside is nothing other than myself.

IV. And yet Merleau-Ponty did not stop there. He set out to recognize and lucidly to interrogate this equivocation, which, as I have tried to show, gives rise to a gliding back and forth between ambiguity and synthesis at the heart of his understanding of dialectic.

This recognition and interrogation will engage the new project, not by way of a pure and simple repudiation of what he had hitherto thought, but by way of a retrieve of the same texts and elected themes in another light. "We must begin everything anew," he wrote in *The Visible and the Invisible*, and this sentence expresses very well the style of his second project. But of its implimentation we have, alas, only scattered fragments. In them one frequently notices the signs of a certain mutation involving, one might say, a displacement of phenomenology towards ontology, of the description of consciousness towards the interrogation of Being, of the humanist and existential *lumen naturale* towards the latency of *aletheia*. Where does dialectic stand in this new context? At the beginning of this paper I suggested that in his final drafts Merleau-Ponty did not repudiate dialectic, but was in search of what he called the 'good dialectic.' If there is a mutation, it does not consist of a thematic replacement, but of a new exploration of the same theme. It is not my intention to follow out this new exploration of the dialectic. I shall restrict myself to indicating those aspects by which it seems to differ from the unquestioning appropriation which we saw at work in the early writings. Most immediately, it is indeed a question this time of an attempt at *confrontation*, and no longer of a practice of encroachment which seeks to expropriate from Hegel and Marx, by hasty analogies, theories in which existentialism may be recognized. There is a genuine effort to interrogate these two thinkers on their own terrain, according to what they said and from the principles which found their discourse. Thus he writes in one of his last texts, the Preface to *Signs*; "To remain faithful to what one was; to begin everything again from the beginning—each of these two tasks is immense . . . one would have to redefine the relationships of the young Marx to Marx, of both to Hegel, of that whole tradition to Lenin, of Lenin to Stalin and even to Khrushchev, and finally, the relationships of Hegelo-Marxism to what had gone before and followed it.'"[7] It is doubtless within this perspective that he had conceived reading texts of Hegel and Marx as his last course.

In the framework of this confrontation we see a questioning of the synthetic ambition of dialectic at work. This is the negative side of this confrontation. It is directed first of all against the synthetic concept of history as the happening of reason, which Marx had invested in the proletariat in his realization-destruction of Hegel, and which Merleau-Ponty had himself earlier retrieved while neither questioning it as such nor interrogating its Hegelian root, since he had envisaged as the primary task of our time the retrieve of an enlarged reason "which goes so far as to integrate the irrational." It is an 'illusion,' he writes in *Adventures of the Dialectic*[8], "to precipitate into a historical fact—the proletariat's birth and growth—history's total meaning, to believe that history itself organized its own recovery, that the proletariat's power would be its own suppression, the negation of the negation" (AD 205). He does not conclude that dialectic is an illusion, but rather that pretension to terminate it in an identity which, precisely because it is pure coincidence without difference or outside, could think itself equally well the culmination of objectivism and the culmination of subjectivism. This is to postulate, he says, the miracle of a directing class gifted with complete coincidence with what it directs, whose movement is without the slightest inertia, and which institutes itself without sedimenting itself; in short, a class which functions in history as "a substantial and given principle which would drive ambiguity from it, sum it up, totalize it, and close it" (AD 221).

Despite this repudiation of the synthetic ambition of dialectic, it is difficult to discover from the book entitled *Adventures of the Dialectic* just what justifies the idea affirmed therein that "the dialectical idea is always valid." Dialectic, as many commentators have remarked, is treated only *ex professo* in several pages of the epilogue. They speak of a dilectic whose site is "the junction of a subject, of being, and of other subjects," or "their communal residence, the place of their interchange and of their reciprocal interpretation," or "the global and primordial cohesion of a field of experience wherein each element opens onto the others;" "dialectic which is not a surpassing centered upon a finality but a "perpetual genesis" to "a plurality of levels or orders" (AD 204).

These remarks are too allusive for one to be able to extract the conclusive indices of a fundamental difference with respect to the concept of dialectic which he had hitherto assumed. Although the confrontation with the world is described as a perpetual, polycentric genesis, this does not fundamentally alter the physiognomy of what had functioned as the privileged domain of the dialectic ever since *The Structure of Behavior*, since here as before it is a question of the reciprocity of Being and the subject, and of the reciprocity of subjects.

But this is no longer true when one turns to *The Visible and the Invisible*. To be sure, there are certain respects in which the text exhibits remnants of the philosophy of subjectivity and of the affiliated conception of truth as adequation between subject and object. The working notes, however, seem to escape the old language of adequation. "We have to pass from the thing (spatial or temporal) as identity, to the thing (spatial or temporal) as difference, i.e. as transcendence, i.e. as always 'behind,' beyond, far-off" reads one of them, and later continues, "Understand perception as differentiation . . . understand that the 'to be conscious' = to have a figure on a ground" (VI 195, 197). Another note makes this more precise: "The for-itself . . . is the culmination of the separation (*écart*) in *differentiation*" (VI 191). The thing as *differentiation*, the for-itself as presence to this differentiation and the locus where it manifests itself—this does indeed seem distant from the classical conception of truth. If dialectic then consists, as several texts suggest, of accompanying and being open to this process of differentiation, it could well be that it had changed meaning along the way. Initially dialectic was supposed to be adjusted to the mode of manifestation of the Gestalt or of the structure of behavior, consisting of circularity between an organism and its milieu, signifying totalization, and negativity. These properties refer, in the final analysis, to consciousness itself as the project of a world, as totalization, as a wrenching from the given. The superimposition of Marxist self-production onto Husserlian intentionality confirmed that the Gestalt was thought within the unquestioned horizon of the modern correlation of subject and object. In the perceived considered as milieu of Gestalten I produce myself and the Gestalt is the objective fact of my project.

But from the moment when the Gestalt, as the final working notes suggest, is less identity than showing-forth, less entity than "operation of *ester*," it situates us "entirely outside of the philosophy of subject and object." Not because it invites us to transcend both in some unity of identity and non-identity, but rather because it bids us welcome the unsurpassable differentiation which it constitutes. Asking himself what is accurate in what he calls the "being for itself of the Gestalt experience," Merleau-Ponty responds, "It is being for X, not a pure agile nothingness, but an inscription in an open register, in a lake of non being, in an *Eröffnung*, in an *offene*" (VI 206-7). If this renovated approach to the Gestalt is indeed at the heart of his last efforts in the direction of a 'good dialectic,' then perhaps the sought-for 'hyperdialectic' rejoins the most ancient sense of *dialegein*: to welcome the difference.

Translated by Robert Crease

NOTES

[1]"Merleau-Ponty. De la dialectique à l'hyperdialectique" appeared in the *Tijdschrift voor Filosofie* 40:1 (March 1978): 34-55.

[2]Maurice Merleau-Ponty, *The Visible and the Invisible*, tr. Alphonso Lingis (Evanston: Northwestern University Press, 1966), p. 94. Subsequent references are identified immediately following quote. Certain of these and other translations have been slightly altered.

[3]Maurice Merleau-Ponty, *The Structure of Behavior*, tr. Alden Fisher (Boston: Beacon Press, 1963). Subsequent references are identified immediately following quote.

[4]Maurice Merleau-Ponty, *Phenomenology of Perception*, tr. Colin Smith (New Jersey: Humanities Press, 1962). Subsequent references are identified immediately following quote.

[5]Maurice Merleau-Ponty, *Sense and Non-Sense*, tr. Hubert L. Dreyfus and Patricia Dreyfus (Evanston: Northwestern University Press, 1964). Subsequent references are identified immediately following quote.

[6]Maurice Merleau-Ponty, *Humanism and Terror*, tr. John O'Neill (Boston: Beacon Press, 1969).

[7]Maurice Merleau-Ponty, *Signs*, tr. Richard C. McCleary (Evanston: Northwestern University Press, 1964), p. 7.

[8]Maurice Merleau-Ponty, *Adventures of the Dialectic*, tr. Joseph Bien (Evanston: Northwestern University Press, 1973).

Merleau-Ponty and the Problem of the Unconscious*

TONY O'CONNOR
University College, Cork, Ireland

I

In the course of a rambling discussion of the character of identity and difference in the *Sophist*, the Stranger reaches a stage where he is able to assert that each thing is both the same as itself, and different from that which is not itself[1]. A problem immediately arises, however, when the attempt is made to predicate existence of these identities, for, although existence may be combined with things, it somehow remains distinct, other, outside the referential system: "And moreover we shall say that this nature pervades all the forms, for each one is different from the rest, not by virtue of its own nature, but because it partakes in the character of difference"[2].

This naming of existence by Plato in Derridean terms as a diverted presentation irreducibly witheld is not unique to the *Sophist*. A similar model is operative in the *Republic* where Plato asserts that the Good, the foundation of things, is both the object of rational knowledge, and outside the system of Being and knowledge altogether[3]. This does not make it a thing-in-itself, or an absent neutrality. On the contrary, it is defection of identity, difference 'without hope of return'[4].

*Paper presented at the Meeting of the Merleau-Ponty Circle, at S.U.N.Y., Stony Brook, October, 1979.

Here the problem arises of how this absent source, this other, is present in human appropriating activity? Paradoxically, it seems that what is grasped in the assertion of justice, truth, harmony, Being, is but a trace of the Good, since the Good is always the beyond, the excess.

No such ambiguity remains in Aristotle. By specifying Being as the fundamental horizon of all discourse he has named what for him is the primary context within which the question of identity and difference may be settled. In the *Metaphysics*, for example, the individual is named as simultaneously a unique existent incapable of being shared by other existents, and as an identity held in common by members of a certain class. Hence, identity is to be established by naming a particular integration in terms of its specific difference from the general class, or from other members of that class. It might even be argued that for Aristotle a principle of selection, or differentiation, is provided by the specification of identity as a unique, single instance of a class.

II

From this admittedly cursory treatment of Plato and Aristotle on the question of identity and difference we have available a certain problematic context within which the discussion of the unconscious may proceed. On the one hand, we have a specification of otherness as outside of presentation; on the other hand, it is available either as a general class, or as an instance of such.

Recent thinkers have begun to approach the unconscious in terms of this question of otherness. Lacan, for example, calls the unconscious 'the discourse of the other'[5]. Derrida claims that for Freud the unconscious is a name for a certain otherness which is definitively taken away from every process of presentation where there might be a demand for it to be shown forth personally[6]. In this context Ricoeur argues that we have a dual problem, for not only is it necessary to articulate the meaning of the unconscious as other, but the very concept of consciousness itself must be rethought and reformulated such that the unconscious can be its other[7].

In phenomenology, particularly as developed under the influence of Merleau-Ponty, stress is laid on the active, intentional behaviour of man in his reciprocal interaction with a human environment. This leads to the view that the unconscious is reciprocal to consciousness in some way. It is a region of the psyche which is present in some manner but which has not yet been brought to explicit consciousness. It is assumed that explicitation will involve an act of gathering, appropriation, or representation, such as a certain cognitional activity, memory, or the sustained investigations of psychoanalysis, which we tend to accept helps in some way to know the essence of the unconscious.

It seems that the unconscious may be specified, therefore, as an element of the human project, or destiny; not as a totally achieved entity, but as an open instrumental field whose implicit and potential character is bound up with the presence of certain signifiers.

If such is the case, then undoubtedly some operator is required, which assures the co-existence of the terms of the relationship in question. One must be present as signifying the other, that is, as rendering the other intelligible, open to thematisation; a thematisation which, in turn, emerges from the situation in which both signified and signifier enter into meaning. Hence, thematisation must always be the correlative of a signifier, a centre of meaning, which is making present both itself and its object.

In Husserlian, and much post-Husserlian phenomenology, consciousness is accepted as the operator, for it is the place or activity where both itself and the unconscious are present within the gathering or thematising activity. Consciousness presents, or represents, both itself and the other than itself.

We see this clearly emergent in Merleau-Ponty's early notion of the lived body, or body-subject. By means of these terms he argues that specification of the psychic in man must admit the entire constitutive complex of inquiring action, which is operative in various modalities, or at various levels. This is to say that human meaning, as fundamental project, must be indicated heuristically. Hence his demand that consciousness be defined not in terms of an apriori, or 'scientific' knowledge of a static self, but by means of what he calls a life of consciousness which transcends its explicit knowledge of itself. On this basis alone, he believes, will it be possible to describe adequately the structures of action and knowledge in which consciousness is engaged (*S.B.*, p. 164).

Thus he argues that if we accept the centrality of meaning, that is, certain intelligible and intelligent structures, it is possible to investigate data in terms of their capacity for action. Such investigation operates in the mode of anticipation and specification, of question and answer, and may lead to the discovery of a characteristic rhythm, or style, in both the investigation and that which is to be investigated. Here we discover the reciprocity of the investigator and the investigated.

Now it seems that we must claim that, within this context, the unconscious is already intentionality, for it is imagined or symbolised in some way. In other words, it is either available to, or heading for, the fulfillment of understanding, as reciprocal to a consciousness which is seen as an active intending open to various perspectival views.

Such a model is intended to overcome a negative ambiguity in the Husserlian endeavour, and to completely reject the basis of Husserl's argument that the unconscious arises by means of passive genesis. This passivity alone, in Husserl's view, permits the unconscious to be present to consciousness without being reduced to the constituting activity of consciousness. In this sense it seems that the unconscious must be a pure passivity, completely non-intentional, without any pretention to knowledge, which is to designate it in Platonic terms as sheer difference, the beyond, the excess, the outside of thematisation, the other.

According to Merleau-Ponty what is neglected in Husserlian analysis is a view of experience as active interpersonal behaviour in which the body is inextricably involved. By overlooking this and by asserting the primacy of passivity it seems that Husserl is in danger of falling into the trap of naturalism which he had tried to avoid in 'Philosophy as Rigorous Science', by according original value to the stimulus before which sensibility is passive.

Against such a possibility Merleau-Ponty argues in his own critique of reflex theory in *Structure of Behaviour* that it is the structure of the organism more than the place or intensity of the stimulus which influences the kind of reaction obtained. This, he claims, prevents the organism from being reduced to the status of a passive receiver, for it is not merely an apparatus, like a keyboard, which permits the production of countless pieces of behaviour depending on the order and intensity of the impulses received. On the contrary, the "properties of the object and the intentions of the subject . . . are not only intermingled; they also constitute a new whole" (*S.B.*, p. 13). Hence, an adequate account must allow for the attentive response of the organism, and not attempt simply to make a determinate content correspond to each partial stimulus. We see this at work, for example, in cases of functional reorganisation of behaviour, where substitute actions, which are put into effect when a member takes upon itself the function of another, occur in a characteristic way only if a vital interest is at stake, and not if a 'made to order' act is involved[8]. In other words, what is involved is not so much the releasing of a local anatomical device, but the means for a return to equilibrium of the entire system.

Thus, even at the level of vital behaviour the organism structures its environment, because in some manner it 'selects' the stimuli to which it will respond, or at very least it is a being which is predisposed to respond to, which 'intends', certain stimuli. This is a kind of proto-understanding, for as observed above, structure is defined as the intelligibility immanent in the configuration so that the value of each element is determined by its function in the whole and varies with it.

Insofar as Merleau-Ponty's critique is an application of the phenomenological doctrine cf *noesis-noema*, we see that on these terms the unconscious must be specified as object of a question, or as content of an act of understanding. In other words, the unconscious is the *noema*; it is open to understanding by the inquirer. But *noesis* and *noema* coincide in consciousness because consciousness is both intelligent and intelligible. The unconscious is not so much a passive presence, then, but an object of an active intending. It must be a part of the system of interpretation, for as what is discovered and known it emerges in the order of the possessed, or the already said. In other words, the distinction between the unconscious and consciousness is not a difference in kind, but between less and more exact knowledge. Hence, it seems that we must reject the Platonic model, which would allow for the unconscious as the outside of thematisation, in favour of the Aristotelian one, and the primacy of consciousness as style of thinking bound up with the attempted rediscovery of my presence both to myself and to my world.

III

While it is commonly accepted that there are justifiable grounds for Merleau-Ponty's rejection of the ambiguities in Husserlian thought, nevertheless, it is argued that still there is room for a discussion of the outside of thematisation. For example, Heidegger talks about the rupture of thematised meaning, and raises the question of how this rupture may be allowed to stand[9]. Similarly, Derrida writes of *'differance'*, which eludes vision and hearing, and which is neither word nor concept.[10] Levinas talks of the trace, as the unsynchronisable which has already preceded the representational activity of consciousness[11].

Within this context it may be valuable to look again at Merleau-Ponty's critique of Husserl. Levinas indicates Husserl's problem well when he says that the unconscious for Husserl possesses an originary and fundamental character not transferable into the question-answer structure. This is achieved by imputing a dual meaning to *erlebnis* as both intentional act and non-intentional content, for by assigning a non-intentional element to sensation he removes it from the realm of knowledge altogether[12]. This region of passivity is sensibility, which includes 'functioning associations' and the processes of consciousness in which the constitution of immanent temporality occurs: "The universal principle of passive genesis for the constitution of all objectivities given completely prior to the products of activity, bears the title association"[13].

Merleau-Ponty's critique of Husserl, then, is a rejection of his associationism, a critique largely influenced by Goldstein's view of sensation. Goldstein argues that what we call 'sensations' are part of a total response pattern within an environment. Common characteristics form a unitary process, the complete pattern of which varies according to the respective perceptual constellations and situations[14]. Hence, the sensory as proto-intention, as preparation for the emergence of a higher meaning, gives the first intimations of the perspectival character of consciousness.

On this basis Merleau-Ponty argues that a theory of association tends to assume that the reasons for correct perception or understanding are given as reasons beforehand (*P.P.*, p. 17). In this respect it neglects what actually occurs in the perceptual or learning situations. It is not the case, for example, that arbitrary data set upon combining into a particular meaning because *de facto* proximities or likenesses cause them to associate, as Husserl seems to think. On the contrary, a grouping is perceived in a particular manner, or a certain set of relations betwen data is understood by the interested inquirer. Association never comes into play as an autonomous force, therefore, but presupposes what it is meant to explain, namely, the patterning of the data, and the imposition of a new order on the flux of the given.

The upshot of this critique is that for Merleau-Ponty the problem of the relation of consciousness and unconscious is a problem of time. For the body is a way of having time, a living presence, a way of overcoming the otherness of that which must be lived from, for in the present Being and consciousness are one (*P.P.*, p. 424). The expansion of the temporal passage to further increments of meaning, and thereby the specification of the unconscious, depends always on interest, motivation, attention etc., for meaning is available only by means of inquiry which emerges from wonder before the world (*P.P.*, pp. 50, 295).

Consciousness as temporal, or dynamic centre of interest, is to be specified now as the concrete establishment of the unlimited fecundity of each present as the product of a culture, but one that will continue to have meaning after its appearance through the opening of a field of investigation in which it may be thematised. This sense of consciousness as self-presence, or self-representing presence, allows for a recovery where, in principle, nothing is lost. It may even be said that a certain priority is given to presence as futural, for in the image the immediate is continually turned toward the search for a more complete presence. Hence, the truth of the event is promised, always future.

IV

Thus Merleau-Ponty may argue that the question of the relation between consciousness and the unconscious is resolvable by a theory of intentional history open to justification insofar as the theory includes the question of the cognitional reduplication of structures, that is, the open-ended construction of wholes from given data. But his reintroduction of the term passive synthesis precisely at the point where he had seemed to reject it entirely, or to reduce it to some appropriating activity, and combined with his self-criticism in both *Phenomenology of Perception* and *Visible and Invisible*, indicates that he is unhappy with the specification of the unconscious as knowable by the inquirer, as available through the activity of recollection, and as able to be situated in the system of one's history.

Now he asserts that the unconscious is the 'other side', the 'reverse', the 'other dimensionality' of sensible being (*V.I.*, p. 255), which is not encompassable by the intentional model. This region is one of both indivision and promiscuity (V.I., p. 253). Commenting on the Sartrean categories of *pour-soi* and *en-soi*, he remarks that the look is one of the givens of the sensible, of the brute and primordial world that not only defies an analysis which gives primacy to consciousness, but requires a complete displacement of philosophy (*V.I.*, p. 193).

What is needed, therefore, is something outside of the relationship of thematised-unthematised which, as observed, is grounded on an appropriating activity engaged in synchronising the phases of the past. He asserts paradoxically that there is need to talk about a fissure that deepens in the exact measure that it is filled:

> . . . the clear vision of being such as it is under our eyes—as the being of the thing that is peaceably, obstinately itself, seated in itself, absolute non-me—is complementary or even synonymous with a conception of oneself as absence and elusion (*V.I.*, pp. 52-3).

Here we witness an implicit assent to the validity of Husserl's problem, for the visible is now called the sensible, or the realm of passivity. It is the world as flesh, the "underlying bond of *non-difference*"

(*V.I.*, p. 261) before division, regeneration, and multiplicity. The unconscious is now made equivalent to the 'reversibility of the flesh', an expression that is meant to designate a realm outside the reflective dimension of the earlier notions of style, historicity etc. In this sense, the unconscious is not a particular object, but the interval, or difference, between objects (*V.I.*, p. 180).

As Ricoeur points out a change in the meaning of the unconscious automatically involves a change in the meaning of consciousness. Now Merleau-Ponty asserts that identity is not the essence of consciousness, which may be viewed no longer as self-presence in the sense of self-transparence. On the contrary, consciousness, as a being of depth, that is, beyond act or intentionality, is opaque to itself.

This break with the presence model, and with absence as its simple symmetrical contrary, is not fully maintained, however, for he continues to call the region of the flesh *"fungierende* or latent intentionality which is intentionality within Being" (*V.I.*, p. 244). Undoubtedly, this realm is not reducible to thematising consciousness, to what Husserl calls 'intentionality of act', nevertheless, insofar as it continues to be interpreted as perception of *gestaltungen*, it remains an 'operative intentionality' (*V.I.* p. 189).

This unwillingness to break completely with the intentionality model is perhaps bound up with his view of language. The formal aspect of language allows the conferring of a meaningful identity upon the temporal dispersion of events, synchronising them into simultaneity. Consequently meaning, time, Being are revealed thematically. The task of language, therefore, is to continually achieve a greater universality, for speech always carries, or intends a representational dimension. Here the unconscious, as bound up with the self-presence of the living present, can be accounted for linguistically. This is particularly true if, with Merleau-Ponty, initiation into language is viewed as a response to the demands of tradition, and insofar as language involves a conventional structure in terms of which verbal phenomena may be thematised, on the one hand; and a propositional character, which relates verbal phenomena back to concrete existents, on the other. But although this permits the conjoining of time and consciousness as language, nonetheless, consciousness remains intentional.

V

Merleau-Ponty's analysis might be said to point back to the primacy of the Heideggerian self-revealing source, and forward perhaps to

Foucault, where the attempt to bypass the personal subject occurs in the assertion that psychoanalysis, linguistics, and ethnology have decentered the subject in relation to the laws of his desire, the forms of his language etc. Man is not master of his desires and his language, but their servant: " . . . questioned as to what he was, (he) could not account for his sexuality and his unconscious, the systematic forms of his language, or the regularities of his fictions"[15].

What is involved here is both a system of temporal dispersion and also a transformable group[16]. In other words, and in Merleau-Ponty's terms, reversibility is time itself, but a time where there is consciousness to the extent that the expression is simultaneously identical with and different from itself. This 'differing in identity' maintains the identity that is altered either as protention or as retention.

On this basis it could be argued that here Merleau-Ponty's notion of passivity returns to the Husserlian *Ur-impression*—original temporality, 'extra-intentional' consciousness, the original source of all Being. In this sense the unconscious is not present, for it does not offer itself in a self-appearing as an object of memory or imagination. On the contrary, it must be evoked in some manner, either from a past, or from some atemporal realm such that it can be said to be presentified[17].

While such a model may appear to overcome the earlier difficulty caused by his use of consciousness as operator, nevertheless, if we consider Levinas' criticism of it we discover that the problem is not so easily resolved. Levinas argues that an 'original creation' is presupposed here, that is, the 'absolute commencement' of every modification produced as time. This originary is not produced itself, but comes to be by spontaneous genesis. Here the region of the real not only precedes that of the possible, but is the definition of the present, and occurs in the mode of consciousness[18].

Insofar as the problem is one of being-present, ontologically it becomes a question of the self-display of Being. The task is to seek a ground of which something can be said, in the sense of the articulation of a principle that allows for the establishment of a relation to Being that forms itself within Being. In this sense the Aristotelian model continues to hold sway, since Being is the fundamental horizon of all intelligibility. As Heidegger argues, for example, without the primacy of Being no thing as such would disclose itself in words, and it would be no longer possible to invoke it and speak about it[19].

Thus we discover that for Merleau-Ponty in *Visible and Invisible* Being is the inner framework of the various modalities of inquiry, and as such is both visible and invisible (*V.I.*, p. 253). It is bound up with the questioning event, which discloses the contextual character of both questioner and source, and permits its reflective articulation (*V.I.*, p. 185). But once again this remains an intentional inquiry insofar as it stems from the fundamental wonder that is selfhood going beyond any achieved integration (*V.I.*, pp. 138-9). Merleau-Ponty's transition to an ontology that rests on dynamic and open-ended questioning activity depends on perceptual faith as he seeks the revelation of the world and its contingent origins. The task of the thinker in this regard is to advert to the primal experience of the world through a series of questions in which he is implicated, and also to situate subjectivity socio-culturally by analysis of how it belongs to an historical world.

Here the unconscious assumes a clearer value, since it is the context from which emerges the constant differentiation of already-established meaning, through the transcendence of the individual into the depth of the visible (*V.I.*, p. 219). In other words, questioning as transcending activity permits the emergence of human contextual self-realisation.

The term 'unconscious', therefore, serves the general claim that all meaning is relative to its context, that situations are open to development or decline, and that we cannot expect complete control of, or certainty about the meaning of the phases of time. To avoid the danger of relativism in this position, Merleau-Ponty insists that he does not stress merely the fact of contingency, but is concerned with the question of whether or not there is something invariant in the operations of questioning itself. As we have seen this is not to argue for the establishment of rigid laws, universal norms, or immutable essences, but to grasp and specify ranges of meanings and values shared communally. It is to argue that historicity and history stem from a directed activity with its temporal changes so that development differs both in individual persons and situations. Man seeks to control his situation and thereby himself by appropriating that control and the techniques which are the means for its realisation.

A break with this model would seem to demand a kind of meaning that is not open to, but beyond, understanding and thematisation. Merleau-Ponty's notions of flesh of the world, perceptual faith, sensibility etc., are open to this kind of interpretation if they are accepted as the indigent corporeity of the living body, which lives as permanent contestation of the prerogative attributed to intentional consciousness in its constitution of meaning as mastery or control. Here the unconscious can be named not as an event of knowledge, but as one of proximity, or pure communication. As the absence of presence it is the very changing of meaning outside the order of representation, or critical consciousness. It is a proceeding toward an end without knowing the end itself, or the means necessary for its attainment.

Insofar as the unconscious is outside the intentionality model, it is temporally present in the mode of lack. And since its ultimate qualitative source cannot be possessed, its mode is insecurity. It indicates self as separated, present as insecurity, since it does not constitute its own meaningful environment, but occurs always in a context of a surplus of meaning, the outside, beyond the capacity of the individual's interiorising activity. It is that which has meaning prior to my donation. But this is the other beyond coincidence and synchronising mediation, yet utterly immediate.

NOTES

[1]Plato, *Sophist* (trans. F.M. Cornford) in: *The Collected Dialogues of Plato* (ed. E. Hamilton and H. Cairns), New Jersey, Princeton, 1963, s. 254d.

[2]*Ibid.*, s. 255e.

[3]Plato, *Republic* (trans. P. Shorey) in *The Collected Dialogues of Plato*, s. 509e.

[4]Derrida, J., *L'écriture et la différence*, Paris, Editions du Seuil, 1967, n. 141.

[5]Lacan, J., 'Of Structure as an Inmixing of an Otherness Prerequisite to any Subject Whatever' in: *The Structuralist Controversy* (ed. R. Macksey and E. Donato), Baltimore, Johns Hopkins, 1972, pp. 186-200.

[6]Derrida, J., *Speech and Phenomena and Other Essays on Husserl's Theory of Signs* (trans. D.B. Allison), Evanston, Northwestern, 1973, p. 151.

[7]Ricoeur, P., 'Consciousness and the Unconscious' in: *The Conflict of Interpretations* (ed. D. Ihde), Evanston, Northwestern, 1974, p. 100.

[8]The dung beetle, for example, after the amputation of one or several phalanges is capable of continuing its walk immediately. However the movement of the stump that remains and those of the whole body are not a simple preservation of the movements of normal walking. Rather, they represent a new mode of locomotion, a solution of the unexpected problem posed by the amputation. Further, this reorganisation of the functioning of an organ is produced only when made necessary by the nature of the surface: on a rough surface where the member, although shortened, can find points of application, the normal process of walking is conserved. It is abandoned, however, when the animal encounters a smooth surface (*S.B.*, p. 39).

[9]Heidegger, M., *On the Way of Language* (trans. J. Stambaugh and P.D. Hertz), New York, Harper and Row, 1971.

[10]Derrida, *Speech and Phenomena*, pp. 129-60.

[11]Levinas, E., 'La Trace de l'Autre' in: *En découvrant l'existence avec Husserl et Heidegger*, Paris, Vrin, 1967, pp. 187-202.

[12]Levinas, E., *Autrement au'être ou au-dela de l'essence*, Nijhoff, The Hague, 1974, p. 79; *En découvrant l'existence avec Husserl et Heidegger*, pp. 116, 149. See also, Keohane (O'Connor), N.M., *The Problem of 'Self-identity' in the Work of Emmanuel*

Levinas, Unpublished Ph.D. thesis submitted to the National University of Ireland, Dublin, 1978.

[13]Husserl, E., *Cartesian Meditations* (trans. D. Cairns), Nijhoff, The Hague, 1960, p. 80.

[14]Goldstein, K., *The Organism*, New York, American Book Company, 1939, p. 230.

[15]Foucault, M., *The Archeology of Knowledge* (trans. A.M. Sheridan Smith), London, Tavistock, 1974, p. 13.

[16]*Ibid.*, p. 127.

[17]Husserl, E., *Formal and Transcendental Logic* (trans. D. Cairns), The Hague, Nijhoff, 1969, p. 141.

[18]Levinas, *Autrement qu'être ou au-dela de l'essence*, p. 42.

[19]Heidegger, M., *Introduction to Metaphysics* (trans. R. Mannheim), New Haven, Yale, 1959, p. 82.

Merleau-Ponty's Examination of Gestalt Psychology

LESTER EMBREE
Duquesne University

MERLEAU-PONTY'S EXAMINATION OF GESTALT PSYCHOLOGY[1]

The thought of Merleau-Ponty has recently moved from being present to being past for us. Among other things, including the passage of time in continental philosophy, this is no doubt due to his posthumous works becoming available and to the maturation of scholarship during the two decades since his death. If he is now a past figure, it is at least easier to subject him to historical study where his development, the internal harmony of the parts and phases of his thought, the influences on and by him, etc. are concerned, i.e. to treat him as having thought in history rather than as having dropped from the sky to challenge us.[2]

The present study contains the results of asking how Merleau-Ponty interpreted, criticized, and developed thought from one of his earliest and largest sources (the present author will deal with the other early large source, Constitutive Phenomenology, in another essay). No doubt there are profounder and subtler gestalty traces in the core of his position than are brought out here,[3] but it seems of importance to study how he dealt with a scientific movement at arm's length, as it were, since this will show something of the assimilative technique as well as the results he gained. The published writings have been worked through chronologically and the several hundred passages where a gestaltist text or author is referred to or a matter is discussed in gestaltist terms noted.[4] Often Merleau-Ponty simply uses Gestalt Psychology approvingly, but often he also discusses it and shows why he accepts and rejects parts of it; hence the word "examination" in the title above. Given the magnitude of this task and the limits of space, it is hoped that merely an interpretation of this examination be accepted in lieu of an examination of it.

Merleau-Ponty read widely in philosophy and science and should be studied for how he relates to Bergson, Brunschvicg, Cassirer, Hegel, Heidegger, Husserl, Marcel, Sartre, Scheler, etc. Where scientists are concerned, some work has been done on the Saussure connection and on Marxism,[5] but work remains to be done on involvements with Freud and other psychologists, with Sociology and Ethnology, and indeed with the Human Sciences in general. Here the concern will be only with the Gestaltists, who for some reason have not received the attention they deserve in Merleau-Ponty studies, possibly because too few in philosophy take science as seriously as he did.[6] Anyone who has read any of his writings knows of this involvement and may even recognize that there is more than can be handled even in only an expository article, unless the Gestalt Physics of Köhler and the Gestalt Physiology (e.g. SC 33-47/33-46) and Psychopathology of Gelb and Goldstein are excluded,[7] in which case the signification of "Gestalt Psychology" in the title above is clearer. Speaking positively, "Gestalt Psychology" refers chiefly to the work of Wertheimer, Köhler, and Koffka, the leaders of the so-called Berlin School of the 1920s, which came to the United States about 1933, but Lewin and the influential French appreciator of Gestalt Psychology, Paul Guillaume, and such convergent investigators as Katz, Michotte, Rubin, and Tolman must also be mentioned.

Before turning to what Merleau-Ponty made Gestalt Psychology out to be, we might survey his thirty-year involvement with it. In the 1920s, Guillaume began writing, translating, and reporting on gestaltist works. It may be that Merleau heard Köhler lecture on "*La Perception humaine*" at the Collège de France in 1929, although the publication of that lecture is not in his bibliographies. When Merleau-Ponty and Gurwitsch met in Spring 1933 the younger man was already familiar not only with phenomenology but also gestaltist thought and even Gurwitsch's dissertation, in which the attempt is made to relate that thought to Husserl's philosophy.[8] That April Merleau-Ponty applied for a grant to study "the experimental investigations undertaken in Germany by the School of 'Gestalttheorie'" (G 9). In February of

1934 he registered the subject of one of his two theses as *La Nature de la perception* and with the same title reported on his research under the grant, refering to some seventeen gestaltist writings. Then in June he registered a title for his second thesis: *Le Problème de la perception dans la phénoménologie et dans la "Gestaltpsychologie"* (G 12 & 188 ff.). By the time he finished writing what came to be called *La Structure du comportement* in 1938, all of the important texts of the Berlin School were known to him.

From the rather abrupt decline in the frequency of references to Gestalt Psychology once Merleau-Ponty had attained the phenomenal field at the end of the Introduction of *Phénoménologie de la perception* (1945), one might believe his interest in it began to decline. However, in his Sorbonne lectures in the early 1950s he went on to discuss Wertheimer's *Productive Thinking* (1945) on the relations of intellection and perception (in a course on the psychosociology of the child!) (BP 213 ff.), increased his appreciation of Lewin's work (BP 112, 116 ff., 159, & 195), and discussed Guillaume's work (BP 161-65). The *Gestaltung* of causation in Michotte's work was also appreciated after the war (P 98, BP 185 ff., cf. RC 14/6); it is unfortunate this work had not preceeded PP, for then that *magnum opus* would probably have had a large place for lived causation. Hence, even though Koffka and Wertheimer died during the war and the Gestalt School, never well transplanted to the United States, was declining, Merleau-Ponty's interest remained strong. *Relatively speaking*, however, it lost its predominance as other lines of scientific thought grew in importance for him. This is most obvious in "Le Métaphysique dans l'Homme" (1947), where Linguistics, Sociology and Anthropology, and History receive comparable attention. This broadening of his reflection on non-philosophic thought is also reflected in his early teaching[9] and was deliberate (P 25 & P 3 ff.) Nevertheless, within the broadening interest the high place for Gestalt Psychology remained to the end (cf. VI 38 ff/20 ff.)

The following exposition has two main parts. In the first, the attempt is made to summarize systematically the concrete gestalt-psychological thought accept by Merleau-Ponty. In the second, the conscious and creative perspective, including the opposition to Gestalt Psychology's naturalistic self-interpretation, a novel frame of reference, and a different standpoint, will be presented. A chronological study of all texts did not reveal any changes in how this thinker, who knew most of the gestalt literature by 1938, comprehended Gestalt Psychology, and hence a synchronic or systematic exposition is legitimate.[10]

I. GESTALT DESCRIPTION

What Merleau-Ponty accepted from Gestalt Psychology without notable transformation can be arranged in relation to three questions: (a) What did he comprehend "gestalt" to signify? (b) Where, with respect to approach, did he believe he was merely agreeing with Gestalt Psychology? and (c) What gestaltist results did he plainly accept? Generally, the focus is on perception, although there are remarks on recollection, emotion, and volition; perhaps imagination was considered Satre's domain.[11] Also, while brutes are mentioned, the focus is also on the human.

A. The Notion of Gestalt

The notion of gestalt is usually expressed in Merleau-Ponty's writings with the word *"forme,"* properly translated into English as "form." For purposes of discussion, however, it seems preferable to use the word *"gestalt(en)"* in a fully naturalized (uncapitalized) way, although "form" will appear in quotations. The word "configuration," presumably from the English candidate which lost out to "gestalt," also occurs.

Since von Ehrenfels, "gestalt" has been frequently defined as a whole not equal to the sum of its parts. Merleau-Ponty repeats this (SC 49/47, SC 163/150), but came to recognize it as merely "a negative, external definition" (VI 258/204). At the outset of his intellectual career he also offered this positive and perhaps internal definition: "The 'Gestalt' is a spontaneous organization of the sensuous field which makes the alleged 'elements' depend on 'wholes' which are themselves articulated into more extended wholes" (G 193). The part/whole characterization is used in other general statements:

> More precisely they are defined as total processes which may be indiscernable from each other while their "parts," compared to each other, differ in absolute size; in other words, the systems are defined as transposable wholes. We will say that there is form whenever the properties of a system are modified by every change brought about in a single one of its parts and, on the contrary, are conserved when they all change while maintaining the same relationship among themselves. (SC 50/47)
>
> Form. . .posses original properties with regard to those of the parts which can be detached from it. Each moment is determined by the grouping of the other moments and

their respective value depends on a state of total equilibrium the formula of which is an intrinsic character of "form." (SC 101/91)

Even in such general statements there is an emphasis on perceptual gestalten: "The form is a visible or sonorous configuration (or even a configuration which is prior to the distinction of the senses) in which the sensory value of each element is determined by its function in the whole and varies with it" (SC 182/168) and "A 'form,' such as the structure of 'figure' and 'ground,' for example, is a whole which has a sense and which provides therefore a basis for intellectual analysis. But at the same time it is not an idea: it constitutes, alters, and reorganizes itself before us like a spectacle." (SC 240/224)

In sum, a gestalt is a whole (*ensemble*) which may be within a larger whole and it has parts, elements, or moments within it such that if all the parts are, say, doubled in size, there is the (specifically) same gestalt, but if one part is changed, there is a different gestalt. Each moment is what it is only in relation to the others within the whole.

Some illustrations may make this clearer. Of course a melody is a gestalt which is preserved when all the notes change in pitch to the same degree. Other gestalten involve movement, rhythm, and spatial arrangement (BP 8). In the last connection, the example can be quite concrete: "The whole of dots

. .　. .　. .　. .　. .

is always perceived as 'six pairs of points two millimeters apart'. . ." (PP 503/440, cf. SNS 86/48). Then again, "the body image [*schéma corporeal*]" is "a global conscious grasp of my posture within the intersensorial world, a 'form' in the sense of Gestalt Psychology" (PP 116/100) and it would seem this description also falls under the definition: "An object is an organism of colors, smells, sounds, tactual appearances which symbolize and modify one another and harmonize [*s'accordent*] with one another according to a real logic. . ." (PP 48/38). In contrast to intellectual contents, Merleau-Ponty repeatedly characterizes gestalten as perceived styles (e.g. BP 180) and especially with the metaphore of physiognomy (see SC 181/166 for a literal usage):

> Beneath the intentionality of the act or thetic intentionality, and as its condition of possibility, we found an operative intentionality already at work prior to any thesis or any judgment, a "*logos* of the aesthetic world," an "art

hidden in the depths of the human soul," and which, like every art, is only known in its results. The distinction which we made previously between structure and signification was clarified thereafter: What makes the difference between the gestalt of the circle and the signification Circle is that the second is recognized by an intellect which engenders it as an area of points equidistant from a center, the first by a subject familiar with his world and capable of grasping it as a modulation of this world, as a circular physiognomy. (PP 490/429, cf. PP 74/60 & PP 441/385)

The above passage also brings us to the contrast of perception and intellection and to the question of whether "structure" is coterminus with "gestalt." In the latter regard, there is of course a close affinity between the notions, such that they sometimes seem synonymous,[12] but Merleau-Ponty usually uses "structure" to designate specifically how a gestalt is organized: "What is profound in the notion of 'Gestalt' from which we started is not the idea of signification but that of *structure*, the indiscernable joining of an idea and an existence, the contingent arrangement by which the materials coming before us have a sense, intelligibility in the nascent state" (SC 223/206, cf. G 193 f.). As has been in part documented above, he uses "structure" in relation to figure/ground organization, but he also refers to other structures (PP 30/22, PP 118/102, PP 257/224, etc.). There can be no doubt of the importance of this notion, especially when as equivalent to "immanent signification" it is contrasted to "ideal signification,"[13] the misunderstanding of which, coupled with the frequent confusion of *"signification"* and *"sens"* in the one English word "meaning," has misled some scholars.

As for perception and intellection, it is already plain that Merleau-Ponty always at least focussed on perceptual gestalten as primary and in the earlier work he goes further: "Hence the form is not a physical reality, but an object of perception; without it physical science would have no sense, moreover, since it is constructed with respect to it and in order to coordinate it" (SC 155/143). "Fixation as a temporal form is not a physical or physiological fact for the simple reason that all forms pertain to the phenomenal world" (PP 268 n./232 n.). At present, what needs to be emphasized is that for Merleau-Ponty gestalten are *not* intellectual forms imposed on sensuous stuffs. This is clearest in the earliest texts we have.

The experimental investigations undertaken in Germany by the school of *"Gestalttheorie"* seem to show . . . that perception is not an intellectual operation,--that it is impossible to distinguish an incoherent matter and an intellectual form there; "form" would be present in sensuous knowledge itself and the incoherent "sensations" of traditional psychology would be a gratuitous hypothesis. (G 9)

This organization [i.e. gestalt] is not like a form which would be placed upon heterogeneous matter; there are only more or less stable and more or less articulated organizations. (G 193, cf. BP 206)

Before shifting focus from this basic category to matters of approach, it may be well to establish that the other extreme from the atomistic sensation is also precluded from Gestalt Psychology as Merleau-Ponty views it. "If everything really depended on everything else, in the organism as well as in nature, there would be no laws and no science. Köhler's whole-processes admit of an internal clevage, and Gestalt Theory stands at an equal distance from a philosophy of simple coordination (*Und-Verbindungen*) and a romantic conception of the absolute unity of nature" (SC 45/43).

With this general conception of gestalt in hand, we can wonder about how gestalten are approachable in research. It goes without saying that this is research on the level of empirical and indeed experimental science, although not of a sort with widespread popularity today, unfortunately.

B. Gestalt Procedures.

When we raise the question of what *approachs* Merleau-Ponty seems to have believed he simply accepted from the Gestaltists, we find three topics. The *first* concerns the relation between internal and external observation. The introduction of this issue is hardly inobtrusive.

A purely objective method can delineate the structure of the universe of "colors" in butterflies by comparing the reactions which are evoked in them by the different colored stimuli—precisely on the condition of limiting oneself strictly to the identity or difference of the responses in the presence of such and such given stimuli and of not projecting our living experience of colors into the butterfly's consciousness. There is an objective analysis and an objective definition of perception, intelligence, and emotion as structures of behavior . . .

. . . .

The mental thus understood is graspible from the outside. Even more, introspection itself is a procedure of knowledge which is homogeneous with external observation.

. . . .

Nothing is changed when the subject is charged with interpreting his reactions himself, which is what is proper to introspection.

. . . .

The object which external observation and introspection intend together is then a structure or signification which is reached in each case through different materials. There is no reason either to reject introspection or to make it the privileged means of access to a world of psychological facts. It is one of the possible perspectives on the structure and immanent sense of the conduct which [is] the only psychic "reality." (SC 197/183, cf. SC 238 f./ 221 f. for relations of this method to Sartre explicitly, Scheler implicitly, the role of language, and the origin of error.)

In SC this doctrine is attributed to Paul Guillaume's "L'Objectivité en psychologie" (1932). That same source is cited in PP (112/95 f.), but only to draw a consequence. In *"Le Primat. . ."* we read, however, that

Without doubt one of the most important acquisitions of this theory has been its overcoming of the classical alternatives between objective psychology and introspective psychology. Gestalt psychology went beyond this alternative by showing that the object of psychology is the structure of behavior, accessible both from within and from without.

. . . .

As Gestalt psychology has shown, structure, *Gestalt*, [sense] are no less visible in objectively observable behavior than in the experience of ourselves—provided, of course, that objectivity is not confused with what is measurable. (P 23 f.)

In BP the point is added that such a compound approach can be taken to oneself as well as to others, for the recourse is to behavior (BP 176), and the attribution is again to Guillaume, although Koffka is credited with a certain transcending of mere introspection as well as of a focus on knowledge (BP 158). Then more is told about the matter thus approachable both from within and without as well as the prejudice which inhibits us from comfortably employing such a two-fold approach.

> The Gestalt Psychologists reveal such a close relationship between perception and motoricity that to dissociate them seems impossible to them: they must be considered two aspects of the *same phenomenon* (cf. D. Katz, *Der Aufbau der Tastwelt*).
> . . . .
> Gestalt Psychology hence obliges us to reconsider the problem of sensation and movement: it is necessary to speak of a perceptual side and a motoric side of conduct, i.e. of two aspects of the same reality.
> It is difficult to make this effort; the classical distrinction is based on deeply rooted philosophic reasons, such as the notion of a contemplative consciousness. The Gestaltists ask us to renounce this conception of a contemplative consciousness detached from action: they replace it with that of an *active consciousness* for which the body is the instrument for exploration of the world. (BP 174, cf. G 185 for passages from "Titres et Travaux" relating the projects of SC and PP to "the junction sought between the objective point of view and the subjective point of view").

If observation from without and from within give access to one and the same phenomenon, there is, in the *second* place, an alternative between procedures more specifically employable within each of these perspectives. This is the alternative of ordinary and analytic attitudes in perception. No particular fuss is made about it in SC, although it would seem assumed in much scientific work. What is the difference?

> I am sitting in my room and look at the sheets of white paper laying about on my table, some in the light shed through the window, others in the shadow. If I do not analyze my perception, but keep to the global spectacle, I shall say that all the sheets of paper look equally white. However, some of them are in the shadow of the wall. How is it that they are not less white than the others? I decide to get a better view [*regarder mieux*]. I fix my gaze upon them, which means that I restrict my visual field. I can even look at them through the cover of a match box, which separates them from the rest of the field, or through

a "reduction screen" with a window in it. Whether I use one of these devices or am contented with observing with the naked eye, but in the "analytic attitude," the aspect of the sheets changes: this is no longer a white paper covered by a shadow, it is a grey or steely blue [*bleutée*] substance, thick and badly localized. (PP 261/225)

Such an alternation can occur also in the spatial perception of size and distance. Ordinarily, one is not aware of such matters as apparent size and occular convergence, which are nevertheless there (PP 298/257), but Gestalt Psychology has shown that they are revealed in analytic reflection (PP 58/47, cf. SNS 87/49, BP 179, S 62/49, & VI 38/21).

Finally, the object in the ordinary attitude has priority over the products of analysis (which are nevertheless not without value) and with respect to such prior objects he can speak of how, "according to the very principles of Gestalt Theory, . . . behavior must be *comprehended* in its immanent law, not *explained* by a plurality of separated causes. . ."(SC 130/120, cf. SC 169/156). Then again, he can write as follows.

> The sensible configuration of an object or a gesture, which the criticism of the constancy hypothesis brings before our eyes, is not grasped in some ineffable coincidence, it is "comprehended" through a sort of appropriation which we all experience when we say that we have "found" the rabbit in the foliage of a puzzle, or that we have "caught" a movement. Once the sensation prejudice has been set aside, a face, a signature, a conduct cease to be merely "visual data" whose psychological signification is to be sought in our inner experience and the psyche of the other becomes an immediate object, a whole charged with immanent signification. (PP 70/57)

In sum, where method is concerned, Merleau-Ponty accepted from Gestalt Psychology that there is one subject matter--"active consciousness" or "perceptual behavior" (a better name could be found, e.g. 'living')--approacheable both from within and from without in oneself and in others, that in approaching such a matter one may have recourse to an analytic attitude, but that the ordinary perceptual comprehension is prior.

C. Gestalt Descriptions.

Under the genus Gestalt fall a number of specific descriptions adopted by Merleau-Ponty without obvious modification. In the first place, for most people, what "Gestalt Psychology" brings to mind is the figure/ground structure and in this respect Merleau-Ponty is no exception. This species of the general organization exhibited in sensuous fields is alluded to him probably a score of times. He accepts from the Gestaltists that it is the simplest sensuous datum, commenting that it is not contingent but rather essential to perception (PP 10/5, cf. PP 81/61, BP 113, & BP 206). A spot, e.g. the dot we use to express a full stop in punctuation, is a case of this (SC 101/92), but the opening example in PP is more richly described.

> Suppose a white patch on a homogeneous ground. All the points in the patch have a certain "function" in common, that of forming themselves into a "figure." The color of the figure is more dense and as it were more resistent than that of the ground; the edges of the white patch "belong" to it and are not part of the nevertheless contiguous ground: the patch appears to be placed upon the ground and does not interrupt it. Each part announces more than it contains and this elementary perception is hence loaded with *sense*. (PP 9/3)
>
> Already a "figure" on a "ground" contains. . .much more than the qualities actually given. It has "contours" which do not "belong" to the ground and are "detached" from it, it is "stable" and of a "compact" color, the ground is unbounded and of uncertain color, it "continues" under the figure. The different parts of the whole-- e.g. the parts of the figure nearest the ground--hence have, beyond a color and qualities, a particular *sense*. (PP 20/13, cf. PP 32/24 & PP 119/102

To this description several points may be added. First, such an account means that our original (*primative*) perception bears more on relations than on isolated terms, these being perceived and not excogitated relations. Second, there must be a greater change in the color of the ground than of the figure for the gestalt to change (G 193, BP 206). Finally, this structure puts attention in a different perspective than is traditional: "To pay attention is not only further to clarify preexistent data, it is also to realize a new articulation in them by taking them as *figures*."[14]

While figure/ground is basic, it should not be overlooked that Merleau-Ponty recognized other species of gestalt structure. That of illumination/illuminated seems next most of interest to him (e.g. PP 354/307) and has its relations with figures/ground (PP 352/305 &

368/323). Furthermore, "the relationships 'figure' and 'ground,' 'thing' and 'non-thing,' [and] the horizon of the past would hence be structures of consciousness irreducible to the qualities which appear in them" (PP 30/22).

Space, especially as seen, is also emphasized by Merleau-Ponty, apparently due to his opposition on to the traditional emphasis on its structures as intellectually imposed. But depth is as intrinsic to what we see as figure/ground and height, breadth, verticality, and obliqueness are *not* established through a mental reference to the meridian of the retina or the axis of the head or body (G 194 f, cf. BP 179). Rather, there are "anchoring points" in our sensuous field which determine the spatial level and there are lines in this field (which is a field of tensions—PP60/48), which are immediately affected with indices of upwardness and downwardness (G 195, cf. SC99/90, PP287/248, BP179). Illumination and the organization of the entire visual field play a role regarding the perceived constancy in size of objects at different distances (PP60f/48 f., PP264f/229, PP351f/305, etc.). Moreover, "Köhler has shown very well that perceptual space is not a Euclidean space, that perceived objects change properties when they change place" (SC156/144, cf. G 196 on "naive statics."). In addition, there is at least a systematic place for temporal gestalten.

> Gestalt Theorists have by no means limited the use of the notion of "form" to the instant or the present. They have, on the contrary, insisted on the phenomenon of form in time (melody). (P 121)
>
> A melody, for example, is a sonorous figure and does not mingle with the ground noises which may accompany it (such as the siren one hears in the distance during a concert). The melody is not a sum of notes, since each note only counts by virtue of the function it exercies in the whole, which is why the melody is not sensibly changed when transposed, that is, when all its notes are changed while their relationships and the structure of the whole remain the same. On the other hand, just one single change in these relationships will be enough to modify the entire physiognomy of the melody. Such a perception of the whole is more natural and more primary than the perception of isolated elements. (SNS 87/49)

Moving things are discussed under the heading of space in PP but plainly involve time as well and Merleau-Ponty is aware of work here by Wertheimer and even Duncker (PP 315 ff./272 ff, BP 180, RC 14/5).

And of course he was aware that separate discussions of seen space and heard time are abstract.

> For people under mescaline, sounds are regularly accompanied by spots of color whose hue, form, and vividness vary with the tonal quality, intensity, and pitch of the sounds. Even normal subjects speak of hot, cold, shrill, or hard colors, of sounds that are clear, sharp, brilliant, rough, or mellow, of soft noises and of penetrating fragrances. Cézanne said that one could see the velvetiness, the hardness, the softness, and even the odor of objects. My perception is therefore not a sum of visual, tactile, and audible data, I perceive in an undivided way with my whole being, I grasp a unique structure of the thing, a unique way of being which speaks to all my senses at once. (SNS 88/50)

More generally, and still without the intellect making any contributions (SNS 91f./51 f.), much of what we have discussed comes under the following description.

> I can at will see my own train or the train next to it in motion whether on the one hand I do nothing or on the other wonder about the illusions of motion. But "when I am playing at cards in my compartment, I see the neighboring train move off, even if it is really mine which is starting; when I look at the other train and look for someone there, it is my own train which is set in motion." The compartment which we happen to occupy is "at rest," its walls are "vertical" and the landscape slips by before our eyes, and on a hill the firs seen through the window appear to us to slope. If we stand at the window, we return to the great world beyond our little world, the firs straighten themselves and remain stationary, and the train leans with the slope and speeds through the countryside. (PP 324/288)

One other passage, in which gestaltist thought is employed on matters of special interest to Merleau-Ponty may be quoted in the present connection.

> The word "here" applied to my body does not designate a determinate position in relation to other positions or in relation to external coordinates, but the installation of the primary coordinates, the anchoring of the active body in an object, the situation of the body in face of its tasks.

Bodily space can be distinguished from external space and envelop its parts instead of spreading them out because it is the darkness in the theatre necessary to the clarity of the spectacle, the ground of drowsiness or the reserve of vague power against which the gesture and its goal stand out, the zone of non-being *before which* precise beings, figures and points, appear. In the last analysis, if my body can be a "form" and if it can have priviledged figures on indifferent grounds before it, this is insofar as it is polarized by its tasks, that it *exists toward* them, that it collects itself in order to reach its goal, and the "body image" is finally a way of expressing that my body is at the world. As far as spatiality is concerned, which alone interests us at the moment, the owned body is the third term, always tacitly understood, in the figure-ground structure and every figure stands out against the double horizon of external and bodily space. One must therefore reject as an abstraction any analysis of bodily space which takes account only of figures and points, since these can neither be conceived nor be without horizons. (PP 117/100)

In sum, it is plain that Merleau-Ponty accepted much in the way of descriptive results as well as procedure from the gestaltists on a fairly concrete level.

II. TOWARD A NEW PHILOSOPHY OF GESTALT

When we turn to the remainder of Merleau-Ponty's examination of Gestalt Psychology, we find interesting efforts at critique, reconstruction, and extension of that thought in a perspective he considered phenomenological. In this higher-level and more creative element, he can be said to have (a) elaborated a frame of reference (to which his discussion on perception and intelligence is closely related) and, after (b) rejecting the naively naturalistic philosophical position the Gestaltists tacitly endorsed, to have (c) reflected on how to regard matters gestaltist from a new and phenomenological viewpoint.

A. Frame of Reference.

At least on the scientific level, Merleau-Ponty's central contribution to Gestaltist thought is his articulation of three species of behavorial structures, the "syncretic," the "*amovible*," and "symbolic" forms. But before this doctrine can be expounded, a crucial issue must be settled. This is the matter of intentionality, which he does not dwell upon in this connection, perhaps because he considered it obvious. If one observes behavior from within and/or from without, there is plainly a difference between the behavior and what is behaved toward in the behaver's surroundings. The related words "structure" and "form" can be applied either to the object "behaved," as it were, by the behaver or the the "behaving" which is under such possibly double observation or, insofar as the matter observed includes the behaving *and* the behaved, both of them. A behaving/behaved distinction is not made in so many words, but it is presupposed in the discussion of the structures of behavior and establishable from what is said in various places:

> *Gestalt Theory* is a psychology in which everything has a sense; there are no psychic phenomena which are not oriented toward a certain signification. In this way, it is a psychology founded on the idea of intentionalty. Only this sense which resides in all psychic phenomena is not a sense which derives from a pure activity of the mind; it is an autochthonous sense which is itself constituted by the alleged elements. (BP 148)

Presumably "signification" here is 'immanent' and thus equivalent to "structure."[15] The same comment applies where Merleau-Ponty speaks of "an authentic phenomenon which philosophy has the function of making explicit. The proper structure of perceptual experience, the reference of partial 'profiles' to the total signification which they 'present,' would be this phenomenon" (SC 233/216, cf. SC 187/172).

Within "The Description of the Structures of Behavior" we find first a mention of the "intentional character, i.e. . . . relation to the situation" in a polemical context whereby it is something overlooked in conditioned-reflex theory (SC 103/93). Then again, in the subsection on *"amovibles* forms," we read that "The behaviors of the preceding category ["syncretic forms"] defintely include a reference to relations" (SC 115/105), and it will be recalled that such relations are in perceptual gestalten (see above, p. 99). "Thus objective description of behavior discovers a more or less articulate structure in it, a more or less rich internal signification, the reference to 'situations' which are sometimes individual, sometimes abstract, sometimes essential" (SC 119/109). Nowhere does Merleau-Ponty say that *all behavior is behavior of* . . . but plainly he could have. In the light of the foregoing we can now interpret the key statement, whereby it is alleged to be possible to classify behaviors "according to whether the structure in them is submerged in the content or on the contrary it emerges from it to become, at the limit, the proper themes of the activity'' (SC 113/103). This is a matter of the structure which is *only intentionally in* the behaving, i.e. is actually a structure of the object behaved. On this basis we can turn to the three species.

Instinctive behavior corresponds (intentionally) to syncretic forms the peculiarity of which is that it is a complex of special stimuli or it is an abstract character of the situation which is reacted to: "if a fly is put in its nest, the spider does not treat it as prey. Its instinctive behavior is not a reaction to the fly but a reaction to a vibrating object in general and it would be initiated just as readily by placing a tuning fork in the middle of the web" (SC 107/97) and "An ant placed on a stick allows itself to fall on a white paper marked with a black circle only if the sheet of paper is of definite dimensions, if the distance from the ground and the inclination of the stick have a definite value, and finally if there is a definite intensity and direction to the lighting." (SC 114/104). Such behavior includes a reference to the relations in the concrete situation and is not, properly speaking, learned. The instinctually "behaved" structures in question are submerged in the perceived objects.

Changeable (amovibles) forms are "relatively independent" of the object (SC 115/105), which seems to mean that they can be established and altered through learning. Köhler's work on chickens shows that again it is a relation, e.g. the comparative colors of sheets with grain on them, which is behaved toward. The emphasis here is first on "sign gestalten" where the subject has learned to perceive something as a means to something else, e.g. color to food. But there are cases where it is an obstacle rather than an access which comes to be seen due to learning and Merleau-Ponty's description can focus alternatively more on the behaving than on the behaved.

> The activity of the organism would be literally comparable to a kinetic melody since any change in the end of the melody qualitatively modifies its beginning and the physiognomy of the whole. It is in the same manner that the closing of an alley in a labyrinth immediately confers a negative value, not only on the entrance to this alley, but on that of a second alley which, after a detour, falls on this side of the barrier; and this is so even if the animal has not just gone through it. The failure has the effect of changing the sign of all the stimuli which have a determined structural relation to the place where it took place. (SC 117/107)

(It might be inserted here that Merleau-Ponty accepts from Koffka that "an object looks attractive or repulsive before it looks black or blue, circular or square" (PP 32/24). There are many subspecies of structures of this sort, Merleau attempts to organize some of them in relation to space and time, but he recognizes the artificiality of this in that "natural structures" have a priority, e.g. a tree branch as something to swing on must be reorganized to become something with which to rake food into one's cage (SC 124/113 f.). There are limits to what brutes can learn, e.g. "the box-as-seat and the box-as-instrument are two distinct and alternative objects in the behavior of the chimpanzee and not two *aspects* of an identical thing" (SC 127/116). It is a "universe of use-objects" (SC 188n.1/245 n.95).

"It is necessary to admit, above the replaceable [*amovibles*] forms available to the chimpanzee, an original level of conduct where the structures are even more available, transposable from one sense to another. *Symbolic behavior* is where the thing structure is possible " (SC 130/120). Signs for brutes are always signals but for humans symbols are also possible. Merleau-Ponty dwells on how activities like piano playing involve intending musical phrases through the instruments (SC131/120), improvisation (even on new types of instruments), and again regards the behaving—behaved situation in a gestaltist manner:

> The character of the melody, the graphic configuration of the musical text, and the unfolding of the gestures participate in a single structure, have in common an identical nexus of signification. The relation of the expression to the expressed, a simple juxtaposition in the parts, is internal and necessary in the wholes.
> . . . .
> The true sign represents the signified, not according to an empirical association, but inasmuch as its relationship to other signs is the same as the relation of the object signified by it to other objects.
> . . . .
> With symbolic forms, a conduct appears, which expresses the stimulus for itself, which is open to truth and to the proper value of things, which tends to the adequation of the signifying to the signified, of the intention and what it intends. Here behavior no longer only *has* a signification, it *is* itself signification. (SC 132 f./121f.).

Corresponding to symbolic behavior there would then be a "spiritual field" (SC 141/131) with "cultural objects" beyond human "use objects" (SC 175/162).

The three-fold classification of behaviors according to the forms they intend can be seen to culminate in the following passage focused on the problem of the differentia of the human.

> What defines man is not the capacity to create a second nature, —economic, social, or cultural—beyond biological nature; it is rather the capacity of going beyond created structures in order to create others. And this movement is already visible in each of the particular products of human work. A nest is an object which only has sense in relation to the possible behavior of the organic individual and if an ape picks up a branch in order to reach a goal, it is because he is able to confer a functional value on an object of nature.
>
> . . . .
>
> For man, on the contrary, the tree branch which has become a stick will remain precisely a tree-branch-which-has-become-a-stick, the same *thing* in two different functions and visible *for itself* under a plurality of aspects. (SC 189/175)

The structures of behavior do not *seem* to play a significant role in PP or in Merleau-Ponty's later writings. The words "symbolic function" come up relevantly (S141/112, cf./140f/122 f.), but not the qualifiers "syncretic" or "*amovibles*." In part this is no doubt due to his not returning to brute behavior, in order words to his focusing on the human. But the thought does appear again in the discussion of intelligence in BP. "Intelligence" appears chiefly to be a matter of problem solving. On the other hand, while Merleau generally deemphasizes the intellect, it should be borne in mind that he did recognize the cogitative, particularly when he argued that the constructs of a gestaltist sort relevant in physics and physiology are modelled on perceptual objects (SC100/91, SC141/131, SC156/144). This is not irrelevant to acts of intelligence in the preeminent signification.

Under the heading of "Relationships between Intellectual Functions and Other Psychic Functions," the general view is that the order of (presumably 'ideal') significations is closely linked to the concrete order of perception. Wertheimer investigated productive thinking from the standpoint of results and conceived of "insight" as the capacity the intelligent subject has of "apperceiving" a signification which will solve his problem in a given figure or situation. "Insight is that by which the given intellectual situation becomes capable of giving rise to a reorganization of the elements it includes" (BP 138, cf. VI 246/192). This is something not every perceiver can do. Köhler showed that chimpanzees must have optical contact with the things which change structure and that their objects cannot have two functions at once, as was just seen to be the case with *"amovible"* forms. Humans can restructure structures and perceive a plurality of aspects to the same thing. Reasoning, moreover, is not only perceiving relationships between two objects but apperceiving a new or third relationship between the two.

> Intelligence is not perception. There exists a difference between the organization of the field in the perceptual act and the reorganization of the field in the intellectual act. — In intelligence the reorganization is not inspired by the same data of perception, but responds to a question which the subject poses. Two structures which succeed one another are not independent, they appear to us two aspects of an identical reality. . . . .—In perception, the structuration is inspired by the data. What suggest this or that transformation are the very properties of the sensible figure. (BP 139)

The same matters are approached in the section called "Transition from Perception to Intellection among the Gestaltists," but the emphasis is on how lower processes of perceptual behavior (which are already intelligent, since problem solving) are transcended by the properly "intelligent" processes. Merleau-Ponty is first concerned to avoid the misunderstanding whereby intellection is considered a species of perceptual gestalt formation (reading *"Gestaltung"* for *"Gestalten"* at BP 210), which certain texts of Wertheimer could stimulate. There is a parallelism between finding the middle term of a syllogism and, for one of Köhler's apes, finding a stick with which to extend one's reach. In both cases there is gestalt formation, but in the case of perception the initial object in effect disappears. In the syllogism, by contrast, what is peculiar is that the three terms remain identical through the varying appearances and even though entering into different relations" (BP 210).[16]

The discussion then follows sensorimotor, animal, and human levels very like the earlier structures of behavior. Both perception and intellection have a sense, "but the sense of the perceived is not the intellectual sense" (BP 211). When a card is moved slightly, the eyes move in order to handle the two images and thus let us go on seeing one spot. "The stimulus does not act upon two symetrical points [on the retinae], but are fused as if, given the analogous function of the two points, the look anticipated the result" (BP 211). Above such sensorimotor problem solving there is an "animal level" where practical intelligence occurs, which humans also have. This is the ability to "replace the signification given an object by another signification" (BP 212; the signification here must be "immanent" rather than ideal). Here the body plays a role in solving problems which are not posed by the intellect. This form of intelligence is not conscious of itself, it is found in habits, not actually those rather rare mechanical ones but in the habit-aptitudes, "those which enable us to respond to situations of the same type by adapted and subtle behaviors (knowing how to dance, knowing how to swim)" (BP 212). This seems the level of *"amovible"* forms.

In peculiarly human intelligence, organization is oriented toward a solution; for example, in geometry, finding the sum of the angles of a triangle or, in algebra, solving an equation of the second degree. In both cases, "its very *form* of the figure (or the equation) which gives rise in me to the idea of a construction to be performed or a theorem to be used. There is a sort of anticipation; one acts for the result one has not yet found; it is not by chance that we are guided by a sort of flair" (BP 212). This constructive character is characteristic. While, secondly, there is little latitude on lower levels, "in the case of an intellectual problem there is a very great number of ways of transforming what is given" (BP 213) and total insight is possible. Thereby a grasping of relationships could be complete in each experience and, independent of varying psychological events, it would tend toward a truth. "When I perceive, I organize my field of experience by utilizing the contingent properties of objects, when I organize intellectually, I utilize general traits, essential and not contingent properties, I retrace an essential dynamism" (BP 213). Intellect differs finally from perception in that there is a recreation and not an adaption of the phenomenal field. Yet the perceived world furnishes us with "prototypes" for intellectual organizations. In short, intelligence is not a species of perception, but it also forms or organizes gestalten, in so doing it is free, unlimited in its ability to contact the true and deal with the essential. It is difficult not to understand this as symbolic behavior.

This frame of reference is elaborated by Merleau-Ponty in a perspective, but for us to understand that perspective and other things he does in it, it will be well to follow his opposition to the perspective in which the Gestaltists did their work.

B. Against Naturalism.

Merleau-Ponty opposes the naturalistic and even physicalistic philosophical assumptions of Gestalt Psychology in two phases, the second more complex than the first. The first phase is prominent in SC but reiterated in BP. Essentially, the view opposed consists in the reduction of psychological gestalten (and one would imagine those of the behaving as well as those of the behaved) to physiological gestalten and thereby to physical gestalten. "Gestalt Theory thinks it has solved the problem of the relations of the soul and the body and the problem of perceptual knowledge by discovering structural nerve processes which have the same form as the psychic on the one hand and are homogeneous with physical structures on the other. Thus no epistemological reform would be necessary and the realism of psychology as a natural science would be definitively conserved." (SC 145/135) Later Lewin, Guillaume, and Koffka are found to have versions of this naturalism (BP 159-61). Merleau-Ponty has several arguments against this view. If there is no structural difference between mental, vital, and physical orders, then there is no difference at all and consciousness would be literally what happens in the brain (SC 146/136 f.). Further, it is not obvious that there are physiological substrata for all behavioral structures, especially the complexes described in Psychoanalysis (SC 83n.1/76 n.93). Finally, for now, only for pathological cases or under laboratory conditions where they are removed from their action contexts are perceptual behaviors explainable with physical models (SC163/150). This reductionism is objected to again in PP (268n./232 n.2).

The more elaborate version of this naturalism is explicated and rejected in relation to the notions of constancy hypothesis and *prejugé du monde*. The critique of the *Konstanzannehme* was accepted by Merleau in 1934, where it is defined as the postulation "of sensations as the primary data of consciousness which one supposes to correspond term for term with the local excitations of the sensory apparatus in such a way that a given excitation always produces the same sensation" (G 192, cf. PP 263/228 & BP 190); because the visual and auditory organs are separate, it is also believed on the basis of the constancy hypothesis that auditory and visual data are separate (PP133/114). To understand this hypothesis and the objections to it accepted by Merleau-Ponty, we need also to grasp the distinction between "geographical" and "behavioral" environments, which can be expressed in a slightly different way: "Koffka distinguishes an objective world, in which all things are in themselves, and a phenomenal world in which things are for a conduct, according to the manner in which I treat the external elements and in which I form [*dessine*] the segregations of objects"[17] According to this distinction, two concepts of stimulus and also of response can be specified. "On analysis, the equivocal notion of stimulus separates into two: it includes and confuses the physical event as it is in itself, on the one hand, and the situation as it is 'for the organsim,' on the other, with only the latter being decisive in the reactions of the animal" (SC 139/129) and "Like that of stimulus, the notion of response separates into 'geographical behavior'—the sum of the movements actually executed by the animal in their objective relation with the physical world; and behavior properly so called—these same movements considered in their internal articulation and as a kinetic melody gifted with a sense" (SC 140/130). This is an illustration: "Two chimpanzees placed in an identical geographical environment, i.e. in a cage where there is a box and bananas which hang from the roof; one then takes the box and uses it to reach the bananas; the other sits on the box.—If the geographic environments are the same, the behavioral environments are different. Immanent in the behavior is a valuing of the box-object now as something to climb on, now as something to sit on." (BP 155)

The gestaltists accepted the distinction between the two environments but not the specification of it whereby there is a one-to-one correspondence between physical stimuli in the objective or geographical world and elementary data called sensations in the phenomenal or behavioral world. The problem with this constancy hypothesis is that the sensations it posits are often difficult if not impossible to observe. "For example, the intensity of a sound under certain circumstances lowers its pitch, the addition of auxiliary lines makes two figures unequal which are objectively equal, a colored area appears to be the same color over the whole of its surface, whereas the chromatic thresholds of the different parts of the retina ought to make it red in one place, orange somewhere else, and in certain cases colorless" (PP 14/7). The sensation is not the only auxiliary hypothesis generated to make the constancy hypothesis work. "Even if what we perceive does not correspond to the objective properties of the stimulus, the constancy hypothesis obliges us to admit that the 'normal sensations' are already there. They must then be unperceived, and the function which reveals them, as a searchlight illuminates objects pre-existing in the darkness, is called attention" (PP 34/26, cf. BP 206). The notion of an unperceived sensation is of course absurd.

Finally, "against the testimony of consciousness, the law of constancy cannot avail itself of any crucial experiment in which it is not already implied, and wherever we believe we are establishing it, it is already presupposed" (PP 15/8). In short, "objective" conditions do not govern the sensuous field part for part.

In objecting to the constancy hypothesis in the above fashion, Merleau-Ponty was not, however, beyond Gestalt Psychology. This school had already performed this critique at its inception. Even so, it still wanted to explain the phenomenal world by means of the objective world. "So we are back in explanatory psychology, the ideal of which has never been abandoned by Gestalt Psychology, because, as psychology, it has never broken with naturalism (PP 58/47). One can respect the integrity of the perceptual gestalt and thus not resort artificially to unperceived sensations and attention and still consider that a gestalt is at least in part the effect of physical events in the objective world. Where Merleau-Ponty goes beyond the Gestaltists is in proposing that something implied not only in the constancy hypothesis but also in the alternative gestaltist explanations with isomorphic physiological and physical gestalten is questionable. This is the *préjugé due monde*, the assumption of an external world or geographical environment which is as natural science tells us it is, even though it is by definition beyond what we can perceive. Justifying that seems a philosophical task not undertaken by the Gestaltists, who were then naively realistic indeed.

C. Description from a New Point of View

In Merleau-Ponty's writings there are many remarks about how Husserlian Phenomenology, as Merleau-Ponty comprehended it, might replace the naive naturalism espoused by the Gestaltists. Fully to interpret what amounts to Merleau-Ponty's examination of phenomenology, including his discussion of Husserl's critique of Gestalt Psychology's psychologism, is beyond the scope of the present study. However, something of the Gestalt Psychology—Phenomenology connection he saw should be dealt with here on the gestaltist side. Koffka is said expressly to have recognized his debt to Husserl (PP 62 n./50 n, P 47) and to have responded in an interesting way to the charge of psychologism: "The description of the 'psyche' in terms of structures, of form, as a vindication of the order of [ideal (?)] significations, would give satisfaction, essentially, to philosophy" (BP 148). Early on, Merleau-Ponty wrote that "one can maintain[18] that Husserl's analyses lead to the threshold of Gestalt Psychology" (G

191). In SC there is call for a new philosophy of gestalt beyond substantialism and causalism (32ff./32ff.) and he writes programmatically:

> To return to perception as to a type of original experience in which the real world is constituted in its specificity is to impose upon oneself an inversion of the natural movement of consciousness;[19] on the other hand, every question has not been eliminated: it is a question of understanding, without confusing it with a logical relation, the lived relation of the "profiles" to the "things" which they present, of the perspectives to the ideal significations which are intended through them.[20]

In PP we are told that criticism of the constancy hypothesis develops, as we have seen, into a critique of the dogmatic belief in the objective world (37/29).

> However, the psychologists who practice the description of phenomena are not normally aware of the philosophical implications of their method. They do not see that the return to perceptual experience, insofar as it is a consequential and radical reform, condemns all forms of realism, that is to say, all philosophies which leave consciousness behind and take as given one of its results—that the real sin of intellectualism lies precisely in having taken as given the determinate universe of science, that this reproach applies *a fortiori* to psychological thinking, since it places perceptual consciousness in the midst of a ready-made world, and that the attack on the constancy hypothesis carried to its logical conclusion assumes the value of a genuine 'phenomenological reduction.'[21]

Just what such a "phenomenological reduction" might precisely signify cannot be discussed here, but it is clear that for Merleau-Ponty Phenomenology means at the very least description of what appears without explanation by means of the external and unobservable factors naively posited in the *prejugé du monde*. If a phenomenological approach encorporating Gestalt Psychological results is therefore descriptive, what more can be said of it? For one thing, it provides allegedly a theory of the kind of reflection which the Gestaltists practiced (PP 62/50). This is difficult to construe, but perhaps it means that in approaching ordinary as well as analytic perceptual behavior from within and from without there is a constant effort to consider objects with respect to how they are for the perception or behaving of them and vice versa. Finally, Merleau-Ponty believed that in a phenomenological standpoint the categories for describing gestalten could be improved. "But what Gestalt Psychology lacks for the expression of these perceptual relationships is a new set of categories; it has admitted the principle, and applied it in a few individual cases, but without realizing that a complete reform of the understanding is called for if we are to translate phenomena accurately" (PP 60/49). Two types of category are reinterpreted by Merleau:

Employing a concept of "motivation" drawn from Husserl and Edith Stein (PP 61/49 & PP 39/31, cf. SC 234/218), Merleau-Ponty endeavors to overcome a failure of Gestalt Psychology to describe the depth of the visual field adequately (Cf. PP 301/259 on apparent shape).

> Gestalt theory has clearly shown that the alleged signs of distance—the apparent size of the object, the number of objects interposed between it and us, the disparity of retinal images, the degree of accomodation and convergence—are expressly known only in an analytic or reflective perception which turns away from the object to bear on its mode of presentation, and that we do not go through these stages in knowing distances. (PP 58/47)

For example, sitting on the bed in a hotel room one might look up and see a church steeple out the window against the sky as rather near, then stand up and, as the other buildings, streets, fields, etc. in between came into view, see the steeple become instead fairly distant. One could sit down again and have the steeple come close once more.

> The objects interposed between us and the thing upon which I fix my eyes are not perceived for themselves; they are nevertheless perceived, and we have no reason for refusing marginal perception a role in the seeing of distance, since, when the intervening objects are hidden by a screen, the distance appears to shrink. The objects which fill the field do not act on the apparent distance like a cause on its effect. When the screen is removed, we see remoteness born of the intervening objects.
> . . . .
> It is not, however, a question of a connection recognized by objective logic, the logic of constituted thought: for there is *no reason* why a steeple should appear to me smaller and farther away when I am better able to see in detail the slopes and fields between me and it. There is no reason, but there is a motive. (PP 60/48)

What then is "motivation"? First we have a general statement and then, deep in PP, a transfer from the traditional situation of how one act (or behavior) motivates another to the interrelationship of moments in the visual field.

> One phenomenon releases another, not by means of some objective efficacy, like those which link the events of nature together, but by the sense which it holds out.
> . . . .
> To the degree that the motivated phenomenon is released, an internal relationship to the motivating phenomenon appears and, instead of the one merely succeeding the other, the motivated phenomenon makes the motivating phenomenon explicit and comprehended, and thus seems to have preexisted its own motive. (PP 61/50)
> What do we understand by a motive, and what do we mean when we say, for example, that a trip is motivated? We mean thereby that it has its origin in certain given facts, not in so far as these facts by themselves have the physical power to produce it, but insofar as they provide reasons for undertaking it. The motive is an antecedent which acts only through its sense and it must even be added that it is the decision which affirms this sense as valuable and gives it force and efficacy. Motive and decision are two elements of a situation: the former is the situation as fact, the second the situation is assumed. Thus a death motivates my trip *because* there is a situation in which my presense is required, be it to comfort the bereaved family or be it to pay "last respects" to the dead and, in deciding to take this trip, I validate this motive which proposes itself and I take up this situation. The relation of the motivating and the motivated is thus reciprocal.
> . . . .
> The enlarged moon on the horizon has long been explained by the large number of interposed objects which emphasize the distance and *consequently* increase the apparent diameter. It follows that the phenomenon of "apparent size" and the phenomenon of distance are two moments of a whole organization of the field, that the first stands to the second neither in the relationship of sign to signification nor in the relationship of cause to effect, and that, like the motivating factor to the motivated act, they communicate through their sense. Apparent size as lived, instead of being the sign or indication of a depth invisible in itself, is nothing other than a way of expressing our vision of depth. (PP 299/258)

To ascertain what is motivating for something motivated, the recourse would seem to be to an analytic attitude. Thus not only would one reflect upon and confine oneself to describing gestalten but one would also on occasion analyze them, although what one thus investigates "phenomenologically" is neither reflective nor analytic itself. "When I look freely, in the natural attitude, at the parts of the field acting on one another and *motivating* this enormous moon on the horizon, this magnitude without measure is still a magnitude. Consciousness must be brought into the presence of its unreflective life within the things and awakened to its own history which it was forgetting, this is the true role of philosophical reflection. . ." (PP 40/31)

In addition to motivation there is another categorical reworking, which can be presented beginning with an example.

> If I walk along the beach towards a ship which has run aground, and the funnel or masts merge into the forest bordering the sand dune, there will be a moment when these details suddenly become part of the ship, and fuse with it. As I approached, I did not perceive resemblances or proximities which finally came together to form a continuous outline of the ship's superstructure. I merely felt that the look of the object was going to change, that something was imminent in this tension, like to storm is imminent in storm clouds. Suddenly the spectacle reorganizes itself, satisfying my vague expectation. Only afterwards did I recognize, as justifications for the change, the resemblance and contiguity of what I call "stimuli"—namely the most determinate phenomena, seen at close quarters, and of which I compose the "true world." (PP 24/17)

This concerns the gestalt laws of Wertheimer, the laws of proximity, resemblance, etc. In Gestalt Psychology, on Merleau-Ponty's view, these terms apply to relations between "objective stimuli," physical things in the "objective" world, the geographical environment. In his phenomenological reformulation of the gestalt laws, Merleau-Ponty first of all has no place for promimity, resemblance, etc. as "objective." But as phenomenal or behavioral, in the second place, these factors require a change of attitude to be grasped, which the passage quoted only begins to indicate. "There are no indifferent data which commence as a whole to form a thing because the defacto contingencies or resemblances associate them; on the contrary, it is because we perceive a whole as a thing that the analytic attitude can then discern resemblances and contiguities."[22]

Where such gestalt laws are concerned, Merleau-Ponty expresses, however, the following reservation.

> Its favorite subject of study was those forms whose appearance, expecially in the laboratory, is more or less regular, given a certain number of external conditions, i.e. the anonymous sensory functions. It was willing to pay any price for precision in their formulae, even if this meant abandoning to some extent the more complex forms which affect the entire personality, are less simply dependent upon given external conditions, and are for that very reason more difficult to discover but also more valuable for the knowledge of human behavior. (SNS149/85, cf. BP245/CAL 62, VI 38f./20f.).

Already in the examples of riding in trains and walking on the beach we nevertheless have seen Merleau-Ponty attempt to use gestaltist thought beyond the laboratory. In writings after PP he applied it also to the film (SNS 85ff/48ff.) and regarding painting, e.g. the distinction between Cézanne and the Impressionists (SNS19f./11f.), presupposes it. In relation to other disciplines he finds matters which he also comprehends in gestaltist terms. Regarding Linguistics, consider these assertions.

> The only reality is the *Gestalt* of language.
> . . . .
> French is not an objective reality which can be sliced up along strict boundaries in space and time; it is a dynamic reality, a *Gestalt* in the simultaneous and the successive.
> . . . .
> Language would not be a *Gestalt* of the movement, but a *Gestalt* in movement, evolving toward a certain equilibrium. Moreover, the *Gestalt* would be capable of losing this equilibrium, once it has been obtained, by a phenomenon of wearing down and of seeking a new equilibrium in another direction. (BP 256/CAL 92-100)

While gestaltist elements are perhaps swamped by structuralism in discussions of Sociology and Ethnology (cf. S 123ff/98ff & S 143ff/-114ff), Merleau-Ponty's treatment of Marxist Historiography is rather interesting. Regarding Freud as well as Marx on the question of why the sense of our behavior might be hidden from us, we are told that "it is not a question of an unconscious which plays tricks; the phenomenon of mystification pertains to how all consciousness is a priviledging consciousness of 'figure' and tends to forget the 'ground' without which it has no sense'' (BP 112). In a much broader way, there is the following statement.

> To be a Marxist is to believe that economic problems and cultural or human problems are a single problem and that the proletariat as history has shaped it holds the solution to that unique problem. In modern language, it is to believe that history has a *Gestalt*, in the sense German writers give to the word, a total process moving toward a state of equilibrium, the classless society, which cannot be achieved without the effort and action of men, but which is indicated in the present crisis as their solution—the power of man over nature and the mutual reconciliation of men. In music a given note on the strings requires a note of the same pitch from the wind and brass; in an organism a given state of the respiratory system requires a given state of the cardiovascular or sympathetic nervous system if the whole is to have the greatest efficacy; in an electric conductor of a certain design the charge at a given point must be such that the whole obeys a fixed law of distribution. In the same way, history, according to Marxist politics, is a system which proceeds by leaps and crises toward proletarian power and the development of a world proletariat, the norm of history, calling for determinate solutions in each domain, each partial change being necessarily retained in the whole. (HT 139f./130, cf. HT 165f./153, SNS 222/126, AD 105/77, and PP 73ff./60f.)

From this it is clear that the reservation regarding gestalt laws and laboratory work quoted above, and also the last and related complaint, namely: "But the enthusiasm is no longer with it; nowhere have we the sentiment of approaching a science of man" (VI 39/21), are about the letter and not the spirit of gestaltist research.

—

In sum, where Merleau-Ponty's philosophical perspective is concerned, we have seen a new frame of reference involving intentionality and structures of behavior in problem solving as well as learning, objections to naive realism in Gestalt Psychology, and some new categories for a descriptive, reflective, and sometimes analytic point of view. For that point of view, gestaltist descriptions are not about the contents of minds conditioned by real but unobservable objects but instead are about the real things which we perceive about us, ourselves and others included.

NOTES

[1] A sketch of this study was read in the symposium on The Philosophy of Maurice Merleau-Ponty at the meeting devoted to French Philosophy in the Twentieth Century of the Society for the Study of the History of Philosophy meeting with the American Philosophical Association in December 1978.

[2] With *Vers une nouvelle philosophie transcendentale, la genèse de la philosophie de Maurice Merleau-Ponty jusqu'à la* Phénoménologie de la perception, The Hague, Martinus Nijhoff, 1971, Theodore Geraets has singlehandedly accomplished a first era of historical analysis on the early Merleau-Ponty.

[3] That there is more going on in Merleau-Ponty's thought than is dealt with here even where the assimilation of gestaltist thought is concerned is perhaps most directly conveyed by this passage. "By a natural development, the notion of 'Gestalt' led us back to its Hegelian meaning, that is, to the concept before it has become consciousness of self. Nature, we said, is the exterior of a concept. But precisely the concept as concept has no exterior and the Gestalt still had to be conceptualized as unity of the interior and exterior, of nature and idea." (SC 227/210)

[4] To save space, time, and energy, the many references offered here are presented textually and in accordance to the usually self-evident abbreviations with initials set forth in the appended list of primary texts. The page number before the slash refers to the French edition used, that after it to the English translation.

[5] See Steven Watson, "Merleau-Ponty's Encounter with Saussure," in *Phenomenology*, Selected Essays from the Husserl, Heidegger, and Merleau-Ponty Circles, publisher being sought, Joseph Bien, "Man and the Economic: Merleau-Ponty's Interpretation of Historical Materialism," *Southwestern Journal of Philosophy*, Vol. III (1972), and Osborne Wiggins, Jr., "Merleau-Ponty and Piaget: An Essay in Philosophical Psychology, *Man and World*, vol. 12 (1979).

[6] The prominent exception here is Martin C. Dillon, "Gestalt Theory and Merleau-Ponty's Concept of Intentionality," *Man and World*, Vol. 4 (1971). On the basis of what is undertaken in the present essay, the present author will discuss Dillon's interesting treatment on another occasion.

[7] Where Gelb-Goldstein is concerned, two passages deserve quotation. "Gelb and Goldstein conclude. . . that the first task, prior to any attempt at physiological interpretation, is to give as exact an interpretation of the morbid behavior as possible. But the experiments to be performed in order analyze the consciousness of the patient would be plainly suggested by the guiding ideas of a psychology of normal perception (in the case of Gelb and Goldstein by those of Gestalt Psychology)." (G 190, cf. SC 70 ff./64 ff.) "The procedures of traditional psychology are strangely mixed with concrete emphasis derived from Gestalt Psychology in the writings of Gelb and Goldstein. They recognize clearly enough that the perceiving subject reacts as a whole, but the totality is conceived as a mixture and touch receives from its co-existence with sight only a 'qualitative nuance,' whereas according to the spirit of Gestalt Psychology two sensory realms can only communicate by being integrated as inseparable moments into an intersensory organization. Now if tactual data, along with visual ones, constitute a whole configuration, it is clearly only on the condition that they themselves, on their own terrain, realize a spatial organization, for otherwise the connection between touch and sight would be an external association, and the tactual data would remain, in the total configuration, what they each are taken to be in isolation—two consequences ruled out

by Gestalt Theory.—It is fair to add that, in another work (*Bericht über den IX. Kongress für experimentelle Psychologie in München,* "Die psychologische Bedeutung pathologischer Störungen der Raumwahrnehmung"), Gelb himself points out the inadequacy of the work just analyzed. We may not even speak, he says, of a coalescence of touch and sight in the normal subject, or even make any distinction between these two components in reactions to space. The purely tactual experience, like the purely visual experience, with its space of juxtaposition and its represented space, are products of analysis. There is a concrete manipulation of space in which all senses collaborate in an 'undifferentiated unity' (p. 76) and the sense of touch is ill-adapted [*impropre*] only to the thematic knowledge of space. (PP 138 n./119 n.).

⁸Personal communication. Cf. Lester Embree, "Biographical Sketch of Aron Gurwitsch," in Lester Embree, ed., *Life-World and Consciousness,* Evanston, Northwestern University Press, for Merleau-Ponty's contact with Gurwitsch, two of whose publications—on Gestalt Psychology and on Psychology and Phonological Linguistics—he helped with linguistically. On the other side of this connection, see Lester Embree, "Gurwitsch's Critique of Merleau-Ponty," *Journal of the British Society for Phenomenology,* forthcoming.

⁹Geraets reports as follows. "In a course on The Foundations of Psychology, taught at the Faculté des Lettres at Lyon in 1945-46, a course the contents of which are known to us through the notes of Mr. Albert Lachièze-Rey, Merleau-Ponty indicates how these three schools lead toward *a new notion of consciousness and of signification.* Freud has shown that all psychic phenomena have a sense [*sens*],—even though the subject rarely grasps it. This signification is not the result of an intellectual and conscious act. Behaviorism shows that consciousness is not knowledge. Gestalt Psychology shows that all of our acts have a structure, of which we are not always conscious." (G 8 n.) See also Hugh J. Silverman, "Merleau-Ponty on Language and Communication (1947-1948)", *Research in Phenomenology,* Vol. 9 (1979).

¹⁰Because the existing English translations are often so inadequate where passages on Gestalt Psychology are concerned, an unusual quantity of freshly translated passages is included here.

¹¹"One could think that in presenting the world as a whole of 'images,' Bergson wanted to suggest that the 'thing' could not be resolved into 'states of consciousness' or sought beyond what we see, in a substantial reality. In a much less precise language, this would be, certainly, an anticipation of the *noema* of Husserl. In the same way, one can find that Sartre is a severe judge of the distinction between matter and form in the image, when he finds it in certain psychologists. . . and too quickly grants to Husserl his distinction of *hylé* and *morphé,*—one of the points of his doctrine which has been challeged even in Germany and offers in fact the most difficulties." (Maurice Merleau-Ponty, "J.-P. Sartre, *L'Imagination,*" *Journal de Psychologie normale et pathologique,* Vol. 33 (1936), p. 761. (The allusion is, of course, to Gurwitsch's work.))

¹²"Psychologists used ["structure"] to designate the configurations of the perceptual field, those totalities articulated by certain lines of force, and where every phenomenon has its local value" (S 146/117, cf. SNS 153/87 & BP 211).

¹³The following is the original key passage. "But, even unknown to us, the true signification of our life is no less the effective law of it. Everything happens as if it oriented the flux of psychic events. Hence it will be necessary to distinguish their ideal signification, which can be true or false, and their immanent signification,—or, to employ a clearer language which we will use henceforth: their actual *structure* and their ideal *signification*." (SC 237/221) Attention has been drawn nicely to this distinction by Claude Panaccio, "Structure et Signification dans l'oeuvre de Merleau-Ponty,"

Dialogue, Vol. 9 (1970). This distinction seems obscure for some Merleau-Ponty interpreters and it would be interesting to read through that *oeuvre* in relation to it.

[14]PP 38/30. "Gestalt Theory has emphasized the existence of a structuration proper to individuals of the categories of adult and child and if one rejects the hypothesis of the constancy of the object, attention finds itself reduced to an abstract name for designating the changes of structuration which intervene in our perception. It is no longer a question of an attention which more or less illuminates an unchanging field but rather of a power of restructuring, of making components of the countryside which did not exist phenomenally appear. Hence there is no longer an illumination of pre-existent details but rather a *transformation of the object*." (BP 131) cf. p. 110 below.

[15]See Note 13 above.

[16]The curious objections to Gurwitsch expressed at BP 210 and BP 214 must be discussed in another context and on another occasion, where Merleau-Ponty's position(s[?]) on ideal objects is thematized. Attention is called on the above matters to Gayne Nerney, "The Gestalt of Problem-Solving: An Interpretation of Max Wertheimer's *Productive Thinking*," *Journal of Phenomenological Psychology*, Vol. 10 (1979).

[17]BP 155, cf. SC 139/129, SC 171/158, PP 94/79, PP130/112, etc.

[18]*Merleau-Ponty's note*: "Gurwitsch, "Phänomenologie der Thematik und des reinen Ich," *Psychologische Forschung*, 1929."

[19]*Merleau-Ponty's note*: "We are defining here the 'phenomenological reduction' in the sense which is given to it in Husserl's final philosophy." Earlier Merleau-Ponty wrote ("Christianism and ressentiment," *La Vie Intellectuelle*, Vol. 36 (1935), p. 288): "We must describe consciousness without prejudice as it appears immediately, the 'phenomenon' of consciousness in all of its original variety. Nevertheless, the claims of a phenomenology of emotional life do not reduce to those of a descriptive psychology. The 'suspension' (*epoché*) of the natural movement which carries consciousness toward the world, toward spatio-temporal existence, and locks it in there [*l'y enferme*], this phenomenological reduction does not only bring about a more accurate [*fidèle*] introspection: it truly introduces a new mode of knowledge, which bears as much on the world as on the ego. For, nevertheless, if we no longer grant any unreflective priority to things, to states of consciousness enmeshed [*engagés*] in space and time, and to the *causal* explanations which they let in, if we follow the articulations of the 'phenomena' within living consciousness, the properties, the connections which they manifest with evidence,—new laws appear to us, there is a necessity which is no longer physical but essential. . . "

[20](SC 236/220) *Merleau-Ponty's note*: "The notion of 'intentionality' will be of help in this regard."

[21]*Merleau-Ponty's note*: "See A. Gurwitsch, Review of *Nachwort zu meiner Ideen* by Husserl, pp. 401 ff."

[22]In "Gestalt Law in Phenomenlogical Perspective" (*Journal of Phenomenological Psychology*, Vol. 10 (1979), the present author has advanced an account which silently encorporates this view but perhaps goes beyond it.

PRIMARY SOURCES USED IN THIS STUDY

Note: Numbers in citations before the slash refer to the French editions and those after the slash refer to the English translations.

AD =   *Les Adventures de la dialectique*, Paris, Gallimard, 1955 / *Adventures of the Dialectic*, trans. Joseph Bien, Evanston, Northwestern University Press, 1973.

BP =   "Maurice Merleau-Ponty à la Sorbonne, Résumé de ses cours établi par des étudiants et approuvé par lui-même, "*Bulletin de Psychologie*, Vol, XVIII (1964). Thus far, only one of these seven courses has been translated (but cf. P, below), namely: *Consciousness and the Acquisition of Language*, trans. Hugh J. Silverman, Evanston, Northwestern University Press, 1973.

EP =   *Éloge de la philosophie*, Paris, Gallimard, 1953 / *In Praise of Philosophy*, trans. John Wild & James M. Edie, Evanston, Northwestern University Press, 1963.

G =   Theordore F. Geraets, *Vers une nouvelle philosophie transcendentale*, The Hague, Martinus Nijhoff, 1971. Texts by Merleau-Ponty contained in this work are "Projet de travail sur la nature de la perception." (1933), "La Nature de la perception" (1934), and quotations from "Titres et Travaux" (1952). The first two of these texts are translated by Forest Williams in *Research in Phenomenology*, Vol. 10 (1981).

HT =   *Humanisme et terreur*, Paris, Gallimard, 1947 / *Humanism and Terror*, trans. John O'Neill, Boston, Beacon Press, 1969.

P =   *The Primacy of Perception*, ed. James M. Edie, Northwestern University Press, 1964. In addition to items subsequently retranslated elsewhere, this title contains translations of "Le Primat de la perception et ses conséquences philosophiques" (1947), "Un inédit de Maurice Merleau-Ponty" (1952), and, in versions slightly different from those in BP, the courses "Les Sciences de l'homme" (incomplete) and "Les Relations avec autrui chez l'enfant" (1950-51); it has not seemed necessary to consult the originals of these translations.

PP =   *Phénoménologie de la perception*, Paris, Gallimard, 1945 / *Phenomenology of Perception*, trans. Colin Smith, New York, Humanities Press, 1962.

PW =   *La Prose du monde*, Paris, Gallimard, 1969 / *The Prose of the World*, trans. John O'Neill, Evanston, Northwestern University Press, 1973.

RC =   *Résumés de cours, Collège de France 1952-60*, Paris, Gallimard, 1968 / *Themes from the Lectures at the Collège de France 1952-60*, trans. John O'Neill, Evanston, Northwestern University Press, 1970.

S =   *Signes*, Paris, Gallimard, 1960 / *Signs*, trans. Richard C. McCleary, Evanston, Northwestern University Press, 1964.

SC =   *La Structure du comportement*, Paris, Presses Universitaires de France, Second Edition, 1949 / *The Structures of Behavior*, trans. Alden L. Fisher, Boston, Beacon Press, 1963.

SNS =   *Sens et non-sens*, Paris, Nagel, 1948 / *Sense and Non-Sense*, trans. Hubert L. Dreyfus & Patricia Allen Dreyfus, Evanston, Northwestern University Press, 1964.

VI =   *Le Visible et l'invisible*, Paris, Gallimard, 1964 / *The Visible and the Invisible*, trans. Alphonso Lingis, Evanston, Northwestern University Press, 1968.

Merleau-Ponty and the Interrogation of Language

HUGH J. SILVERMAN
State University of New York at Stony Brook

To interrogate language is to raise the question of its place and meaning within the frame of human experience. Maurice Merleau-Ponty never ceased to interrogate language; but in asking about language, he reformulated its character into four generally synchronic knowledge frameworks. Within what he called the primacy of perception, he wove a texture of problematics, including nature, thing, body, world, time, freedom, dialectic, art, history, and vision. Each problematic implicates and incorporates the others. Language is inscribed within the texture of problematics as the disclosure of their relationships but also according to the knowledge frame in which they operate.

Merleau-Ponty returned to the question of language again and again—from its initial formulation in *Phenomenology of Perception* (1945) to the version offered in his posthumous and unfinished *The Visible and the Invisible* (1964). Within each framework, he would retrace to a certain degree the terrain he had already traversed and each time he would reformulate his understanding of language. In each reiteration, the shape of language as a problematic itself had changed. Yet there are no radical epistemological breaks along his itinerary and there is no continuity of thought either. As he articulated his understanding of language, it underwent significant transformations in the almost two decades during which it played a role in his thinking and writing.

The framing of the four formulations includes (1) the language of the body [1945], (2) the philosophy and psychology of communication [1946-52], (3) indirect language [1952-57], and (4) the language of visibility [1958-61]. Because these frameworks incorporate texts resulting from formal lectures and uncompleted manuscripts as well as deliberate publications, a certain overlap in the dates of appearance mark the organization of texts.[1]

I shall offer a three-fold reading of the four formulations. The first and most extensive reading establishes Merleau-Ponty's appropriation of language according to the four different frameworks or formulations. The second reading offers an interrogation of language based upon its appropriation within Merleau-Ponty's own enterprise. The third reading takes the interrogation of the appropriative and appropriated language to its limits, to the place at which it no longer operates simply as a lived language of significations. This last reading moves to where its own paradoxes of expression locate a style which is not in any particular place but which ajoins, corners, and signs the inscription and interpretation of particular languages—of literature, of corporeity, of history, of sociality, etc.

For each of the four formulations, a distinctive, diacritical, and oppositive relation characterizes the appropriateness of language. The elaboration of the oppositional structure is already the interrogation of language. The elaboration does not simply announce the appropriateness of language, for it places itself in the between, at the locale in which language is questioned, where language is neither a philosophical construct nor a practical tool, where language becomes a system of significations with a style of its own. For language to have a style of its own is to take language too far, to take it to excess. For language to rely exclusively on a network of significations is to underestimate language. The limits of language occur at the juncture, at the intersection, at the cornering (*accointance*) where the ambiguity of significations[2] meets the expression of a style. This placement of language at the limits of significations on the one side and the achievement of style on the other constitutes the parameters which Merleau-Ponty announces but cannot fulfill.[3]

I. THE LANGUAGE OF THE BODY

In the *Structure of Behavior* (1942), Merleau-Ponty found little place for language. The critique of early behaviorism, the building of the human order onto the vital and physical orders, and even the relations between body and soul circumvented the question of language.

As far as the structures of behavior were concerned language seemed inappropriate. Because the concept of structure was identified with the notions of form and *Gestalt*, structure in the sense of de Saussure's structural linguistics did not enter into Merleau-Ponty's considerations until soon after the publication of *Phenomenology of Perception* [1945]. Indeed, in 1946, Merleau-Ponty taught a course at the Ecole Normale Superieure on Saussure. In the following year he published his essay "The Metaphysical in Man," where he not only mentions de Saussure but also ascribes to him the view that the speaking subject lives in his language.

Between *The Structure of Behavior* (1942) and "The Metaphysical in Man" (1947), the appropriateness of language was intimately bound up with Merleau-Ponty's account of the body, particularly as the region of expression and speech. The body is transfigured by expression and speech. The dichotomy between subject and object is no longer in question, for the body appropriates meaning (*sens*) for itself in the act of speech. The speaking subject carries speech through its bodily gestures prohibiting a disincarnated consciousness. Consciousness is already corporeal and speech is already the incorporation of meaningful thought. In speaking, in gesticalating, in articulating, in signaling, the body is the locus of meaning production. Thus the body of the word, which is incorporated into speech, is the material instrument of verbal expression.

In this first formulation signalled by *Phenomenology of Perception*, Merleau-Ponty distinguishes two kinds of speech: *parole parlante* and *parole parlée*.[4] The opposition is critical; for between "speaking speech" and "spoken speech," speech appropriates its meaning. All thought is speech in a certain respect. Thought attains a body, it becomes a language when it is spoken through speech by a speaking subject. In other words, between the speaking and the spoken is a language. The language in question here is nothing other than the language of speech (*parole*). But speech is already body—the experiential use of phonatory organs, the singing of music, the reciting of words, the expression of ideas, the articulation of objects, etc. Speech announces itself as the body in action—what it produces is a "spoken speech" (*parole parlée*),—its producing is "speaking speech" (*parole parlante*). The production of spoken speech by speaking speech is the constitution of language—the assembly of meanings in order to create signification, a signifying intention which is necessarily already corporeal.

Speech of the sort I have been considering remains within the domain of verbal language; this speech produces words, sounds, and utterances. However another dimension of this phenomenal field in which language is proper to the body, in which the body is appropriate to language, is gesture. Gesture is the paradigmatic case of bodily expression. Yet Merleau-Ponty does not begin with gesture; he does not make other forms of language derivative of the gestural. In both speech and gesture, the body becomes thought, the body inscribes meaning in a texture of experience by which it speaks—not in words but in movement and in a tendency toward expression. Signalling to a friend to "come here" in Italian, shrugging one's shoulders in French, frowning in British English, and indicating quotation marks in American are all forms of gesture. They all tend toward expression. They all demonstrate the movement of thought through the living body. Such gestures are tied to specific cultural contexts and therefore partake of what seems arbitrary and conventional as in a verbal language. Even though some may claim that gestures or emotional imitations are natural signs (as Merleau-Ponty suggests) nevertheless they operate within a nature/culture opposition where natural signs are conventionalized and conventional signs are naturalized. What is eminently important here is that whether one is offering an elaborate philosophical discourse, asking the price of a beer, saying "no" with one's hands, fingers, shoulders, and head, or laughing out of joy, the body is the medium of expression. All expression is both bodily and the *topos* of meaning production. As Merleau-Ponty puts it, "the human body is defined in terms of its property of appropriating in an indefinite series of discontinuous acts, signifying kernels which surpass and transfigure its natural powers."[5] In going beyond its natural limitations, the body adopts a tendency toward cultural expression, toward a language (*un langage qui devient une langue*). This movement of the body proper (*le corps propre*), of one's own body is itself already the appropriation of language, making language one's own in order to speak, in order to express oneself.

But without other people (*autrui*), there would be no need to express oneself. The appropriation of language is already a movement of reciprocity, a tendency toward communication. Speaking is already a gesture which carries with it a meaning just as gesture carries its own meaning.[6] This orientation toward communication occurs in the attempt to grasp and transmit meaning, to fulfill the reciprocity between my gestures and those of others. It is "as if the other's intention inhabited my own body and as if my intentions inhabited his."[7] This contextualization of gesture, and speech which is already gesture, indicates, elaborates, and inscribes a texture for the appropriation of language.

II. THE PHILOSOPHY AND PSYCHOLOGY
OF COMMUNICATION

Although Merleau-Ponty introduced the question of communication in *Phenomenology of Perception*, he thematized it in the years following the war, in the years which saw the formation of *Les Temps Modernes*, in the years when he was teaching first at Lyon and also at the Ecole Normale Supérieure de Paris and then as a professor of psychology at the Sorbonne. In the span of about five years (from 1945 to 1950), Merleau-Ponty discovered structural linguistics, incorporated it into his phenomenological perspectives and addressed himself even more intensively to the problem of language and particularly that of communication. As he had already demonstrated in his principal doctoral thesis (*Phenomenology of Perception*), the appropriation of language incorporates communication. By extending his critique of Gestalt psychology, behaviorism, and psychoanalysis within the shadow of both Husserl and Saussure, he entered upon a consideration of the philosophical and psychological aspects of communication.

In his 1945-1946 Lyon course, he began a systematic study of theories of language in Western philosophy from Heraclitus, Socrates, and Plato to Descartes, Berkeley, and Locke, and on to Humboldt and Cassirer.[8]

In the 1947-48 lectures on language and communication,[9] he develops his critique of scientisms in psychology, sociology, history, and linguistics in order to establish the relationship between language and thought and to articulate the role of the speaking subject in communication. The evidence of both schemes or structures and the temporal evolution of language indicates Merleau-Ponty's adoption of the synchronic and diachronic elements of structural linguistics. Both of these aspects are actualized in the speaking subject. At no time can this appropriation of language by the speaking subject allow language itself to become an object—even for the linguist, who must speak in order to carry on his enterprise. For Merleau-Ponty, the intentionality of language places thought within language such that "I rejoin myself in speaking."[10] The words that I speak are "surrounded by a halo of meaning." The philosophy of language must go beyond the pure phenomenon of language in order to appropriate it and in order for its appropriateness to take place.

In his first formulation concerning language, Merleau-Ponty did not recognize the symphonic character of language. It is corporeal, but it also has temporally changing structures. This synchronics and diachronics of language offers a framework for the experience of speaking subjects. In order to translate the experience of speaking subjects into an experience of communication, Merleau-Ponty turned to Husserl's fifth cartesian meditation. Unfortunately this threw him back again into a problem of my nihilation of others as they nihilate me in that the other's subjectivity becomes an objectivity for me and vice versa. In order to go beyond this theory of mutual objectification, which recurs in the early Sartre, Merleau-Ponty appeals to the notion of intersubjectivity as the coupling of my speech with the speech of others; hence producing communication. The difficulty which Merleau-Ponty faced was that in order to obtain a communicative appropriation of intersubjective language, he could not remain within the transcendental model which Husserl offered. De Saussure's structural considerations helped to establish the conditions for both temporality and communicability, but they could not be fully reconciled with the Husserlian perspective. He had already shown in his brief discussion which covers a few pages of "The Metaphysical in Man" that Gestalt psychology establishes a "communication between and a mixture of the subjective and the objective."[11] but Gestalt psychology is inadequate in this respect. It only sets up the possibility of the conjunction of Husserlian phenomenology and Saussurian structuralism. The linking of these two orientations seemed to be a natural outgrowth of Gestalt psychology's concerns with both intentions and structures. But as Merleau-Ponty gradually discovered, he could only incorporate the models by transforming them into an existential and developmental context. Intentionality could no longer remain transcendental and structure could no longer imply "form," "whole," "figure against a ground." The appropriation of communication would have to remain a "desire" until he could free himself fully from both the problematics of "intersubjectivity" and "holism" without at the same time falling into the formal models of structuralism. Thus he wrote in 1947:

> "That general spirit which we all constitute by living our life in common, that intention already deposited in the given system of language, pre-conscious because the speaking subject espouses it before he becomes aware of it and elevates it to the level of knowledge, and yet which only subsists on the condition of being taken up or assumed by speaking subjects and lives in their *desire for communication*—this, in this field of linguistics, is indeed the equivalent of the psychologist's form, equally alien to the objective existence of a natural process as to the mental existence of an idea."[12]

The formulation of communication as a "desire" could be attributed to a variety of interests which both informed and plagued Merleau-Ponty's early work. The "desire for communication" cannot be realized because of the aporias of the Husserlian theory of transcendental subjectivity, because of the search for comprehension in forms which Kohler, Koffka, Gelb and Goldstein proposed, because of the unrealizable libido ever present in Freudian psychoanalysis, and because of the Sartrian theory of mutual objectification which Merleau-Ponty could never quite overcome.

Yet in his courses for the Institut de Psychologie at the Sorbonne in 1949-1952, he sought avenues whereby the theory of communcation could become appropriated into the experience of language. In *Consciousness and the Acquisition of Language*, he stressed the developmental account of language in order to uncover the manner in which a child learns to speak and communicate. This important approach which has been followed through by cognitive psychologists but which has been left largely untouched by phenomenologists, stresses linguistic diachrony—not in terms of the history of languages, but in terms of an individual person's acquisition of a language and his communication with others. Merleau-Ponty traces the child's path from babbling to the appropriation of linguistic structures including the acquisition of phonemes and the imitation of others. He was particularly interested in how children more than seven years old communicate with each other and was dismayed with Piaget's conclusion that "there is no true communication between children."[13] Piaget's limited conception of "comprehension" forces him to draw conclusions which prohibit a full description of communicative relations among children. By examining the pathology of language, he could demonstrate how in cases of verbal hallucination and aphasia, there is indeed a shrinkage of the child's appropriation of language and the possibility of communication.

Although the language which Merleau-Ponty explores in this second formulation is limited more specifically to verbal language, the language of the very young child certainly incorporates gestures which are not yet those of the speaking subject. But even if it is possible for the child to appropriate language, that is, to make it his or her own, it is more difficult for the child or even the adult to appropriate communication. Thus Merleau-Ponty turns from psychological and pathological theories to the philosophical implications of linguistic theory. Saussure's views occupy an even greater place in *Consciousness and the Acquisition of Language* than in earlier writings. The diacritical aspects of language indicate differences: conceptual differences on the side of the signified, phonic differences on the side of the signifier. And the sign itself which is composed of the signifier/signified opposition is an arbitrary relation—a relation which is itself conventional. Because the arbitrary nature of the sign results in a differential linguistic system, "each linguistic phenomenon is a differentiation of a movement of communication."[14] While "value" can be exchanged for an infinite number of objects, "signification" remains an essential part of a particular communicative experience. On the basis of signification, the communicative experience spans, intertwines, and appropriates the conventional system of differences. In the articulation of signs, he writes, "each speaking subject finds himself reintegrated into the collectivity of speaking subjects. The *global will* to communicate with the *alter ego* founds the positive [aspect] of the linguistic phenomenon. But this linguistic phenomenon, considered instant by instant, is never anything but negative, diacritical. The currency for a global possibility of communicating makes up the very essence of the speaking subject."[15] Communication is appropriated only by a will, as a possibility, as the speaking subject reintegrates himself into the collectivity of speaking subjects—that is, as the speaking subject inscribes himself in the system of differences which constitutes a language.

In the year following his course on *Consciousness and the Acquisition of Language*, Merleau-Ponty began a two year course on "Phenomenology and the Sciences of Man." The English version of the text is only partial but it does include the section in which Merleau-Ponty took up the role of linguistics in Husserl's philosophy. In returning to Husserl, Merleau-Ponty is again faced with the problem of rescuing the experience of language, of liberating the speaking subject, of achieving communication among speaking subjects by avoiding the trap of an objective study of language. The phenomenologist is concerned with what the speaking subject really is, with an elaboration and adoption of language as it is spoken. "The speaking subject is turned toward the future. Language for him is above all a means of expression and of communicating to others his intentions, which are also turned toward the future."[16] This access to a speaking subject in the later Husserl is no longer a concern with a transcendental subject but with a speaking subject in a definite linguistic situation. As Merleau-Ponty puts it, "to know what language is, it is necessary first of all to speak. It no longer suffices to reflect on the languages lying before us in historical documents of the past. It is necessary to take them over, to live with them, to speak them. It is only by making contact with this speaking subject that I can get a sense of what other languages are and can move around in them.''[17] In this respect Merleau-Ponty viewed Husserl as approximating the task which Saussure had set before himself: to return to the speaking subject in its linguistic context—which for Husserl is a fullness and for Saussure a system of differences. Whether it accounts for the appropriation of identity as in Husserl or the appropriation of difference as in Saussure, the appropriation itself, the making of a communicative situation in which language is lived as one's own is the formulation of Merleau-Ponty's enterprise in this second version.

The final account of this version was made clear in one of Merleau-Ponty's last courses before moving on to the Collège de France in 1952. In *L'Expérience d'autrui* (1951-52), he distinguishes clearly between a language (*une langue*) and language (*le langage*). The language which concerns him is not a language (*une langue*) such as French, German, or English, but *"le langage* as a phenomenon of communication.''[18] An interpreter employs language (*le langage*) in order to communicate a movement of thought. But, in fact, this communicative language is already the inscription of a system of significations, a system of differences which passes from language to what is meant: the sign is already structuration and structuration is already a system of significations which constitutes the communicative situation.

III. INDIRECT LANGUAGE

By building a link between Husserl and Saussure, Merleau-Ponty opens up the field not only of the desire and possibility to communicate, but also the appropriation of a language which is not direct, not fully explicitated, but which speaks and which is communication itself. This is the indirect language which Merleau-Ponty examines in "Indirect Language and the Voices of Silence" (published in *Les Temps Modernes*, June and July 1952).

Retracing the steps he had left in the form of lecture notes, Merleau-Ponty reiterates the child's efforts at communication even on the level of babbling. He reiterates the importance of the Saussurian theory of the sign and he moves toward the meaning which arises at the edge of the sign, at the outskirts of the system of linguistic differences. Brunelleschi builds the cupola to the Florentine cathedral in conformity with its site. He does not accomplish his task by making references to explicit architectural signs. Rather he envelops them with an appropriative action, a speech of sorts in which Brunelleschi the architect announces the full meaning of the context. It is as if he could communicate with the site in order to fulfill its meaning:

> A language sometimes remains a long time pregnant with
> transformations which are to come; and the enumeration
> of the means of expression in a language does not have any
> meaning, since those which fall into disuse continue to lead
> a diminished life in the language and since the place of
> those which are to replace them is sometimes already
> marked out—even if only in the form of a gap, a need, or a
> tendency.[19]

Further on Merleau-Ponty adds: "The meaning occurs at the intersection, in the interval between words." Thus when the meaning does
arise, it fills in the gaps which were already marked out, already
prepared for expression. In other words, language itself is indirect,
allusive—silence. Indirect language prepares the way for speaking,
writing, painting, etc. In this third formulation of the appropriation
of language, language denies the presence of pure meaning, language
opens up a field of differences in which significations that appear as
guide posts begin to take shape. To appropriate indirect language is to
bring about meaning in the intervals between significations (based on
signs) which begin to appear in expression. Language for Merleau-
Ponty is not only the movement toward communication but also the
fulfilling of expression through the appropriation of differences in the
verbal chain and through the identification of significations which we
grasp in terms of a broad movement toward expression. In this third
formulation, Merleau-Ponty builds upon bodily gesture and the desire
to communicate, the tendency toward expression through an indirect
language. The appropriation by the writer or painter of the indirect
language is like the child's orientation toward speech, toward the acquisition of a conversation (and hence an intersubjective language.) Yet it
also carries with it an originating intention, a genesis of language out
of silence, a "tacit language"—the field of speech before it is spoken.
    Malraux's concerns with the development of perspective in paint-
ing, when incorporated into the lessons Merleau-Ponty has reaped
from Husserl, Saussure, and the Gestaltists, establishes the domain out
of which bodily expression can become communication through art.
When the voices of silence speak, they speak through paintings such as
those of Cézanne, Klee, and Van Gogh, through the writings of Stend-
hal, Valéry, and Proust—. An operant and latent meaning becomes
manageable for the artist. It establishes a field of expression that, once
appropriated by the artist, begins to generate meaning out of which its
significations can be appropriated by others.
    In this third formulation, in the years from 1951 to 1954, Merleau-

Ponty draws upon his earlier study of Cézanne's experience and gives it a context as the indirect language through which meaning and hence signification can arise. As he puts it, "when one goes from the order of events to the order of expression, one does not change the world; the same circumstances which were previously submitted to now become a signifying system."[20] "The human use of the body is already primordial expression,"[21] which means that when Renoir paints his *Bathers*, his understanding of the body takes on expression in his painting. It is not simply the representation of bodies, but also the meaning of bodily expression which begins to speak through the painting as a signifying system—a framework of significations which the art historian can articulate but which the spectator appropriates in his or her own experience. In this way, culture adopts significations through the incorporation of human meanings. The process of expression gives rise to arts of expression. The artist destroys ordinary vision by realizing it just as the writer defeats the constraints of ordinary language by realizing it.[22] Or in another version, "language speaks and the voices of painting are the voices of silence."[23] The appropriation of a language which can say: "These beautious things have not been to me as is a landscape to a blind man's eye" as Wordsworth does, or the appropriation of the corporeal visible as Renoir does in *The Bathers* are the speaking of a language and the voices of silence as they enter the expressive texture of what Husserl called "intersubjectivity." Both Wordsworth and Renoir conventionalize, culturalize, and bring the indirect language into a corporeal language of communication.

In the posthumous *Prose of the World* (written primarily between 1950 and 1952), Merleau-Ponty develops even further this experience of expression. The intention to communicate (the problematic of Merleau-Ponty's second formulation) is now oriented toward the transformation of meanings into a system of expression. The painter for example paints as much by the lines he traces, the blank spaces on the canvas, and the brush strokes he does not make as much as the specific shapes he fills in. This indirect visual expression has its analogue in the truly expressive speech of the poet and prose writer. In embarking upon *The Prose of the World*, Merleau-Ponty set out to respond to Sartre's *What is Literature*? (1947) as Roland Barthes did in his *Writing Degree Zero* (1952). He hoped to provide an account of literary experience in which communication is a central feature, but which is not simply grounded in the communication of freedom by the prose writer. The writer's task is, as he elaborates in the chapter on "Indirect Language":

> to choose, assemble, wield, and torment these instruments in such a way that they induce the same sentiment of life that dwells in the writer at every moment, deployed henceforth in an imaginary world and in the transparent body of language.[24]

Merleau-Ponty is far more concerned with "the sentiment of life that dwells in the writer" than with the priority of prose over poetry and the specific audience of writers. Indeed he is closer to the Heideggerian problematic which becomes more and more significant in his writings. Just as Heidegger seeks to think the writer's language as the opening up of a speaking of language which situates itself in the ontological difference, similarly Merleau-Ponty emphasizes the writer's dwelling in a significant texture of differences which cuts horizontally across the writer's contact with the world through his speech. That Merleau-Ponty associates the experience of the writer with that of the painter necessarily undercuts the dichotomy which Sartre establishes between the poet who is like Tintoretto painting a yellow sky as opposed to the prose writer like Malraux who is engaged in a definite situation and whose goal is the freedom of all mankind. Here again Merleau-Ponty approaches a Heideggerian meditation which brings together the experience of Van Gogh's peasant shoes with a Greek temple and Hölderlin's poetry. Thus when Merleau-Ponty writes that "all of classical painting rests on the idea of a communication between the painter and his public through the evidence of things,"[25] he is announcing and appropriating a language—an indirect language—which allows for the communication of painter and public through the embodied experience of things in the world.

Again and again within this third formulation Merleau-Ponty distinguishes the algorithm or a pure language from the literary and other types of indirect language. He rejects the ideal of a "successful" language which can stand disembodied from experience. Even the orientation toward the achievement of a universal language is continually situated within an experiential expression. The algorithm, for Merleau-Ponty is "a revolt against language in its existing state and a refusal to depend upon the confusions of everyday language."[26] The search for pure signification is the attempt to overcome the gaps, intervals, and differences in the experience of language. In the algorithm, communication is only an appearance and never actually brings anything new. Despite its project of escape from the indirections of language and its attempt to appropriate language within a fully circumscribed and completely opaque system of knowledge, it, in fact, appropriates only a very small, limited, and direct aspect of experience. Algorithm expression remains simply secondary; it can be *exact* because it can accomplish precisely what it sets before itself as its task. It does not require appropriation because it is already proper to itself and only to itself.

In offering itself to literary language, the algorithm can avoid the problems inherent in passing from the sensible world to the world of expression, for the algorithm is pure, limited, and direct expression. It has no need of painting itself with the sensible—which, for Merleau-Ponty, is already involved in the enterprise of the creators of a universal language. By contrast, literature is in advance of the philosophy of language. Literature already incorporates and highlights the miracle of the mystical union of sound and meaning, signifier and signified. In his 1953 Collège de France lecture on "The Literary Use of Language" Merleau-Ponty builds upon what he described as the "mystery of language" in the *Prose of the World*. The mystery of language—"indirect language" is a more fortunate formulation for what Saussure characterized as an arbitrary relation between signifier and signified—indicates the difference or gap which is distributed throughout expression and highlighted particularly in literature. Freud's notion of the "overdetermination of speech"—which Lacan has identified with metaphor—is another form of the expressive appropriation of language through which meaning fills the differences and sets up a system of significances. Literary speech expresses the world, so too does the overdetermined language of the patient reporting a dream. "Perhaps all men, as well as the man of letters, can only be present to the world and others through language; and perhaps in everyone language is the basic function which constructs a life and its work and transforms even the problems of our existence into life's motives."[27]

IV. THE LANGUAGE OF VISIBILITY

The fourth formulation of Merleau-Ponty's considerations on language emerges in the last two years of his life (between 1959 and 1960)—depending upon when he actually began writing *The Visible and the Invisible*. These considerations also include his last published work *Eye and Mind* and several brief remarks in his last course *Philosophy and Non-philosophy since Hegel*.

The problem which inserts itself into any examination of these texts, and particularly that of *The Visible and the Invisible*, is one of interpreting an enterprise which opens onto an ontology of difference, but which itself tends toward novel expression. In short, how can the language of visibility appropriate itself to its own enterprise. Without a doubt, Merleau-Ponty continues to build upon his prior appropriations: gestures and incarnate speech realize the orientation toward communication and the rounding out of indirect language. But a new question is raised in the last years: how can the interrogation of Cartesian reflection, Hegelian and Sartrian dialectic, Husserlian and Bergsonian intuition open up onto the chiasm, an intertwining which is both the difference and identity of the visible and the invisible, the seen and the see-r, the touched and the touching.

The chiasm is a vertical, ontological relation. In one working note, Merleau-Ponty associates it with the "ontological difference"[28]—which is so commonly associated with Heidegger. The ontological difference, the chiasm of visible and invisible, the intertwining of seeing and seen, touching and touched establishes an invisibility which is filled only by perceptual faith, which achieves meaning only in the appropriation of a language of visibility. It would seem however that this type of visibility could be articulated without stressing the place of language. It would seem that the reciprocity of visible and invisible might not necessarily appropriate language. It would seem that the difference enacted in the intertwining need not enter into speech. But when we remember that *la chaire* (flesh) establishes visibility, which fills out the body and its surroundings, it becomes evident that once again language speaks in the ontological difference, in the chiasm, in the unachieved gap between the visible and the invisible. The *écart* is opened up and appropriated in language along with the meaning which literature, music, and even the passions give it. The reversibility of the visible and invisible is also the invisibility of speech and what it signifies.[29] The signification which arises out of this vertical relation between speech and its signified is elaborated horizontally across a system of differences—the system of differences which Merleau-Ponty discovered when he appropriated the structural linguistics of de Saussure. This horizontal movement, continually opening up new horizons, cuts across the vertical *écart*, sets itself up as language and enters into an ongoing communicative movement within the intercorporeity of the interworld (*intermonde*). Thus meaning arises out of the vertical difference; a system of significations arises out of the horizontal differences; and language is appropriated in the intersection of the vertical difference and the horizontal differences.

These horizontal differences are not the object of a reflection from above (a bird's eye view of things, a *pensée de survol*), nor are they the result of a series of things which distinguish themselves from each other. The horizontal differences are proliferated at the membrane, hinge, juncture, cornering (*accointance*) of visible and invisible—they are the proliferation of speech across a whole, moving field of differences. The note which ends with *"langage et chiasm"* demonstrates Merleau-Ponty's commitment to this double crossing of difference as a fundamental orientation in which the appropriateness of language is indicated. The appropriation of language is the appropriation of flesh.

Thus the painter who adopts a fleshly understanding of the world is able to make the object he sees visible in the painting. In *Eye and Mind*, Merleau-Ponty cites Valéry as saying that the painter "takes his body with him,"—and he adds "not the body as a chunk of space or a bundle of functions but that body which is an intertwining of vision and movement."[30] The painting is the silent articulation of the intertwining of "essence and existence, imaginary and real, visible and invisible—a painting mixes up all our categories in laying out its oneiric universe of carnal essences, of effective likenesses, of mute meanings."[31] In this respect, Cézanne's Mont St. Victoire does indeed demonstrate the silent speech with its mute meanings which Merleau-Ponty described in his third formulation through the work of Malraux. What is different in this fourth formulation is that painting is a demonstration of visibility and an appropriation of a language which gives access to the structure of Being, a polymorphous Being with multiple dimensions. Language here is based on painting with its proper essence of the visible, and its doubling of the invisible. "This mute Being which speaks in painting has its analogue in the figurations of literature and philosophy—the only privilege of speaking—thought," Merleau-Ponty writes "is to have rendered its own support manageable."[32] He suggests thereby that speech operates with a similar access to Being, a similar ontology that situates itself in the fleshly difference between the spoken and the unspoken, in the *écart* of speaking. That it is possible to appropriate the language of philosophy in a similar fashion is the topic of Merleau-Ponty's last course *Philosophy and Non-Philosophy since Hegel* (1961).[33] By identifying the difference between philosophy and non-philosophy, the appropriative dimension of philosophy is the dimension of experience in all its ambiguity.

V. INTERROGATING LANGUAGE

This essay is entitled the interrogation of language. So far the inquiry has restricted itself to the appropriation of language. Without an elaboration of what is proper to language, it cannot be interrogated effectively. Without an indication of language—as bodily gesture and speech, as communication, as the indirect expression of literature, painting, and music (by contrast to the algorithm), and lastly as an ontology of visibility and the intersection of differences,—without the building of formulation upon formulation, the full interrogation of language cannot even be proposed. This means that what is proper to language (including speaking, writing, and painting), what belongs to language, and what language can call its own—once elaborated with care—enters into each formulation with an interrogative mood.

Interrogration is a dominant thematic of Merleau-Ponty's fourth formulation. He offered a course on the topic in 1959. In this course, he noted that he would concern himself with the possibility of philosophy in 1959. Interrogation situates questioning in the between, at the juncture, on the hinge. Interrogation opens up and makes what is philosophical in language (or whatever is to be interrogated) speak for itself. When interrogating philosophy itself Merleau-Ponty sought to indicate how philosophy becomes non-philosophy in the present age.[32] In this respect philosophy interrogates its own meaning and possibility—that is, it situates itself in the difference between philosophy and non-philosophy, in the system of differences which are marked by significations. Philosophy interrogates the *Ineinander* of Being in its difference from beings.

The interrogation of language situates itself as a direct repetition of the appropriation of language. The interrogation of language questions the already said of the appropriated in order to examine its meaning, it significations, and ultimately its limits. The interrogation of language asks language about its meaning and possibilities. In order to fulfill the enterprise, each of the four formulations must be reviewed one by one—each must be interrogated as a unique epistemological framework which is itself layered and stratified in order to produce an ontology of language, an ontology which establishes its own limits.

The itinerary of interrogating language in Merleau-Ponty identifies four distinct thematics: (1) ambiguity (2) lived language, (3) the orientation toward expression, and (4) the paradoxes of expression. Each is built upon an opposition, a difference which allows for the articulation of the interrogation and the meaning of its placement.

In the first formulation, which is characterized by ambiguity (i.e. the multiplicity of meanings held in tension within the phenomenal field of the body),—the opposition between speech and expression prevails. Speech is a form of gesture which achieves meaning through its conjuncture with expression. The insertion of ambiguity between

speech and expression announces the opening of a field in which verbal meanings are already experiential, in which gestural meanings are
already expressive. Ambiguity is the production of a corporeal
multiplicity whose interrogation announces the significance of perception in its most general characteristics.

The interrogation of the second formulation installs itself in the opposition between linguistics and the speaking subject. What is appropriate to language in this second formulation is the contribution of
linguistics, particularly that of Saussure, but also Jakobson, Goldstein, Vendreys, Guillaume and others. Structural linguistics
demonstrates that language is founded on a system of differential relations which gives rise to significations. On the basis of such a system,
the child acquires a language and tends toward communication, which
is also the orientation of adults. The acquisition of a language, the expression of linguistic structures, and the establishment of intersubjectivity in terms of language is already accomplished by the work of
the speaking subject. The speaking subject gives meaning(s) to
linguistic science such that what arises out of the interrogation (in the
difference) is a *lived language*. The lived language supplants and
augments the thematic of ambiguity in the first formulation.

In the third formulation, the difference between the algorithm or
pure language and indirect language establishes (through interrogation) the movement toward expression. Expression is not a given. It
arises only out of a field of silence which is given to speaking through
painting, poetry, prose, music, etc. This indirect language opposes
itself to the universal, pure language which is sought after by an objective, exact science of language,—by a science which reduces differences to positivities,—by an enterprise which seeks to ignore the
voices of silence. Nevertheless out of the opposition expression
becomes possible.

The still groping, but more fully articulated form of this possibility
occurs in the fourth formulation in which the tendency toward expression is replaced by the paradoxes of expression. Expression has its
multiple directions, its intertwinings and criss-crossings in the differences between visible and invisible, touching and touched, in the
flesh of the chiasm. There the logos of the sensible world remains
meaningful and ontologically fulfilling of the expressive dimension of
corporeality which is already intercorporeality and of intercorporeality which is already an interworld where expression takes place. In this
respect the ambiguity of experience is a lived language which is
oriented toward the achievement of the paradoxes of expression.

Significantly, and here I conclude—at least temporarily—in each of the four formulations, the place of style always stands at the edge, at the margin of the appropriation and therefore in the interrogation. Style has no definite place in the ambiguous field of bodily speech and expression—yet Merleau-Ponty announces its appearance as "Spinozist, criticist, and phenomenological."[35] Style is a certain way of linking up with the natural world, a manner of speaking or even singing the world. Thus each gestural signification appropriates a style all its own. But the appearance of that style unrewinds (or deconstructs) the generality and the singularity of the expressive situation.

In the orientation toward communication, style appears in the differential structure of significations. "Style is defined neither by words nor by ideas," it possesses an oblique rather than a direct signification.[36] It announces the arrival of the "new." Thus the child imitates the style of the speaking subject and not the words themselves. Style is our "manner."[37] It is the quality of the ambiguous meanings of experience as it inscribes itself in the significative differences of language. As a text the system or horizontal differences tend toward signification. Style is the tendency toward signification in the lived language.

In the movement toward expression of indirect language, style identifies itself at the limits of language. The child adopts a "style of expression" in order to speak. Similarly style "germinates at the surface of the artist's experience"[38] where his system of equivalences begins to take on its own particular characteristics. Style is simply the speech of the voices of silence.

But finally, the allusive, elliptical style of the fourth formulation remains inimitable, inalienable and inbetween the inner and outer horizons of a visibility that seeks to express itself in all its multiple and paradoxical aspects. The countryside of fleshly experience, as Merleau-Ponty states in *The Visible and the Invisible*, is only a variation on speech. To speak of its "style" is to create a metaphor.[39] Style is already metaphorical of speech. Style is the paradox of expression taken to its limits. Style is the crossing out of both the ontological difference and the differential system of significations in the intertwining of the visible and the invisible. Style is visibility without either identity or difference.[40]

NOTES

¹James M. Edie has listed Merleau-Ponty's writings on language in his "Foreword" to *Consciousness and the Acquisition of Language*, trans. Hugh J. Silverman (Evanston: Northwestern University Press, 1973), pp. xi-xxxii. Since Edie's listing is incomplete due to subsequent publications, I offer a full accounting according to the four framework formulations announced in this essay:

(1) The Language of the Body

[1945] "The Body as Speech and Expression" in *Phenomenology of Perception*, trans. Colin Smith (London: Routledge and Kegan Paul and Atlantic Highlands: Humanities Press, 1962), pp. 174-199.

(2) The Philosophy and Psychology of Communication

[1947] "The Metaphysical in Man" in *Sense and Non-Sense*, trans. Hubert L. Dreyfus and Patricia A. Dreyfus (Evanston: Northwestern University Press, 1964), pp. 83-98.

[1947-48] "Language and Communication." Lecture course at the Université de Lyon (summarized and discussed in Hugh J. Silverman, "Merleau-Ponty on Language and Communication: 1947-1948," *Research in Phenomenology*, Vol. IX, pp. 168-181).

[1949-50] *Consciousness and the Acquisition of Language* (cited above).

[1950-51] "Phenomenology and the Sciences of Man," trans. John Wild in *The Primacy of Perception and other essays*, ed. James M. Edie (Evanston: Northwestern University Press, 1964), pp. 43-95.

[1951] "On the Phenomenology of Language" in *Signs*, trans. Richard C. McCleary (Evanston: Northwestern University Press, 1964), pp. 84-97.

[1951-52] "The Experience of Others." Lecture course given at the Institut de Psychologie, Sorbonne.

(3) Indirect Language

[1952] "Indirect Language and the Voices of Silence" in *Signs*, pp. 39-83.

[1950-52] *The Prose of the World*, ed. Claude Lefort, trans. John O'Neill (Evanston: Northwestern University Press, 1973).

[1953] "The Sensible World and the World of Expression" in *Themes from the Lectures*, trans. John O'Neill (Evanston: Northwestern University Press, 1970), pp. 3-11.

[1953] "Studies in the Literary Use of Language" in *Themes from the Lectures*, pp. 12-18.

[1954] "The Problem of Speech" in *Themes from the Lectures*, pp. 19-26.

(4) The Language of Visibility

[1959-61] *The Visible and the Invisible*, trans. Alphonso Lingis (Evanston: Northwestern University Press, 1968).

[1960] "Eye and Mind" trans. Carleton Dallery in *The Primacy of Perception*, pp. 159-190.

[1961]   "Philosophy and Non-Philosophy since Hegel," trans. Hugh J. Silverman, *Telos* No. 29 (Fall 1976), pp. 43-105.

²See my article "Merleau-Ponty's Human Ambiguity," *Journal of the British Society for Phenomenology*, Vol. 10, No. 1 (January 1979), pp. 23-28.

³See my essay "Re-reading Merleau-Ponty," *Telos* No. 29 (Fall 1976), pp. 106-129 for an indication of what the fulfillment of such an enterprise might entail.

⁴*Phenomenology of Perception*, p. 197. In the original Gallimard edition (Paris, 1964) p. 229.

⁵Ibid., p. 193. (Fr., p. 226).

⁶Ibid., p. 184. (Fr., p. 214).

⁷Ibid., p. 185 (translation altered). (Fr., p. 215).

⁸See my "Preface" to *Consciousness and the Acquisition of Language*, p. xxxvii.

⁹See my "Merleau-Ponty on Language and Communication (1947-48)," *Research in Phenomenology*, Vol. IX (1979), pp. 168-181.

¹⁰"Merleau-Ponty on Language and Communication (1947-48)," p. 174.

¹¹"The Metaphysical in Man," in *Sense and Non-sense*, p. 86.

¹²Ibid., p. 88 (my emphasis).

¹³*Consciousness and the Acquisition of Language*, p. 58 [Henceforth cited as *CAL*].

¹⁴*CAL*, p. 98.

¹⁵*CAL*, p. 99.

¹⁶"Phenomenology and the Sciences of Man" in *Primacy of Perception*, p. 81.

¹⁷Ibid., p. 83.

¹⁸"*L'Experience d'autrui*" [The Experience of Others] in *Bulletin de Psychologie*, 1950-51, p. 623.

¹⁹"Indirect Language and the Voices of Silence" in *Signs*, p. 41.

²⁰Ibid., p. 64.

²¹Ibid., p. 67.

²²Ibid., p. 79.

²³Ibid., p. 81.

²⁴*The Prose of the World*, p. 48.

²⁵Ibid., p. 50.

²⁶Ibid., p. 5.

²⁷"The Literary Use of Language" in *Themes from the Lectures*, p. 18.

²⁸*The Visible and the Invisible*, p. 270. (Fr. p. 324).

²⁹Ibid., p. 154. (Fr. p. 202).

³⁰"Eye and Mind" in *Primacy of Perception*, p. 162.

³¹Ibid., p. 169.

³²Ibid., p. 189.

³³See "Philosophy and Non-Philosophy Since Hegel."

³⁴See my "Re-reading Merleau-Ponty".

³⁵*Phenomenology of Perception*, p. 179. (Fr. p. 209).

³⁶*CAL*, p. 31.

³⁷*CAL*, p. 42-43.

³⁸"Indirect Language and the Voices of Silence" in *Signs*, p. 53.

³⁹*The Visible and the Invisible*, p. 155. (Fr. p. 203).

⁴⁰An expression of gratitude is owed to the faculty and students at the 1979 *Collegium Phaenomenologicum* (Perugia, Italy), where this essay was composed and first presented, and to those who offered helpful comments when it was delivered as an invited lecture at University College, Cork (Ireland), The University of Essex (England), and Georgetown University (USA) early in 1980.

Pretexts:
Language, Perception, and the Cogito in Merleau-Ponty's Thought

STEPHEN WATSON
Colgate University

In the preface to the *Phenomenology of Perception* Merleau-Ponty renders an account of language and perception in which the subject enjoys an immediate grasp of the presence of the given. Language is not a screen impervious to thought in its relation to the perceived world, but the treasure reflecting an engagement with the things themselves. In reference to a characterization by Jean Wahl of the distinction between essence and existence in the works of Husserl, he states:

> Husserl's essences are destined to bring back all the living relationships of experience, as the fisherman's net draws up from the depths of the ocean quivering fish and seaweed. Jean Wahl is therefore wrong in saying that 'Husserl separates essence from existence.' The separated essences are those of language. It is the function (*fonction*) of language to cause essences to exist in a state of separation which is in fact merely apparent since through language they still rest upon the pre-predicative life of consciousness. In the silence of originary consciousness (*conscience originaire*), one sees appearing not only that which words mean but likewise that which things mean: the core of primary signification (*signification*) around which acts of denomination and expression are organized. (Ph.P.: xv/x)[1]

Language is, therefore, the mirror image, the apparent state, of a silent core, or to use Sartre's term, an "infrasilence,"[2] that is more primordial than it. It is, in fact, the re-presentation of this silence in a form of abstraction, of separation. As such, it is the holder of a meaning received and imparted from another domain, a domain "furnishing the text which our knowledge tries to translate into precise language" (Ph.P: xviii). In short, the world is what we perceive, and what we perceive gets translated into words. Thus, on this account there is a strict relation between our knowledge and the original or 'pre-text' (since it is the "core" to which all signs ultimately refer) to the perceived world. And, as a result of this relation the sign is granted a status which remains always derivative.

The work that stands behind this paper is the result of a Fulbright/Hays fellowship for study in Belgium. Special thanks for his time and assistance are offered to Professor Jacques Taminiaux of the University of Louvain as well as Professors Lester Embree and Hugh Silverman who read and commented on this paper at various stages of its development.

Merleau-Ponty explicates this standpoint with regard to the "essence of consciousness:"

> Whatever the subtle changes of sense (*sens*) which have ultimately brought us, as a linguistic acquisition, the word and concept of consciousness, we enjoy direct access to what it designates. For we have the experience of ourselves, of that consciousness which we are, and it is on the basis of this experience that all linguistic significations (*significations*) are assessed, and precisely it which makes (*fait que*) language mean (*veut dire*) something for us. (Ph.P: xv/x).

Here I come upon an actual presence to self beneath the *level* of the universe of things said. And it is precisely here, at this Archimedean point where, as he put it, "I am the absolute source" (Ph.P: ix), that language not only undergoes assessment, but becomes meaningful. In the return to the things themselves that this preface on the nature of phenomenology reinstates, then, the elements of knowledge can be cleanly separated on the basis of this direct means of access into "the world which precedes knowledge, and of which knowledge always speaks (*parle*)" and the 'speaking' which remains "significative (*signative*) and *dependent*" regarding it (Ph.P: ix/iii).

The secondary status that significative practices receive in the preface is part and parcel of the Cartesian leanings of classical phenomenology. One can witness it, for example in § 124 of *Ideen I* where Husserl states:

> The stratum of expression—and this constitutes its peculiarity—apart from the fact that it lends expression to all other intentionalities is not productive. Or if one prefers, its productivity, its noematic service exhausts itself in expressing . . . [3]

Here the sign is understood as the sheer reflection of the pre-linguistic stratum of sense (*Sinn*). In itself it remains void of significance and adds no substantial content to the one it re-presents. For Husserl it becomes meaningful only through the constitutive expressive acts underlying it. Closer to Merleau-Ponty, a similar standpoint can be witnessed in the early work (at least) of Sartre. In a polemic against Brice Parain who had argued for the priority of the sign over the 'immediate,'[4] Sartre responds:

> . . . the word has no privileged stature. For I must also make (*fasse*) the table and the tree and the white worm exist as permanent syntheses of relatively stable properties. It is not by naming them that I endow them with objectivity. But I can name them only if I have constituted them as independent wholes, that is, if I objectify the thing and the word that names it in one and the same synthetic act. [5]

The subject must constitute the things and words mutually as *objects*. How could a sign intervene in this primordial relationship in which objects can arise as designated in the first place? How could there be an intervention without the intervened designatum being always already prior to its sign? It is, then, under the objectification of a reflective gaze that sign and signified are conjoined. This finds confirmation again in the considerations on intersubjective communication in *Being and Nothingness*, despite the fact, as Dominick LaCapra has noted in his book, *A Preface to Sartre*,[6] that it is only seldom that Sartre has faced the problem of language head on. In a rare text concerning language intersubjectivity, and knowledge of the lived body, Sartre states:

> Nevertheless, it is necessary to realize that it is not on the unreflective plane that language with its meanings can slip in between my body and my consciousness which exists it . . . In order that any knowledge which the Other has of my body and which he communicates to me by language

may give to my body-for-me a structure of a particular type, it is necessary that this knowledge be applied to an object and that my body already be an object for me.[7]

The sign again remains *dependent*, to use Merleau-Ponty's category, with respect to the signified, derivative in relation to the immediate presence of subject to object, a presence on the basis of which it can then be made meaningful. In this regard subject and object, sign and signified, the layer of silence intrinsically meaningful and its contrary, all must be rigorously distinguished and a strict logical and ontological order established among their elements. In this sense these classical 'phenomenologies' are in mutual agreement: language and perception are similarly and rigorously distinguished.

II.

The writings of Merleau-Ponty that have been considered thus far have all been taken from the preface to the *Phenomenology of Perception*, a writing added to the book following its completion at the insistence of Brunschweig. There is a sense then in which these statements could be taken as the author's final word on the subject at the time of its composition. This claim could go unchallenged, however, only if it were consistent with or explained the position proffered in other relevant passages in the *Phenomenology*.

First, Merleau-Ponty's emphasis in the chapter on the body as expression and speech makes this assertion problematic. The chapter opens by specifying the importance of the analyses which are to follow. "In trying to describe the phenomenon of speech and the specific act of signification (*signification*), we shall have the opportunity to leave behind us, once and for all, the traditional subject-object dichotomy" (Ph.P: 174/203). As becomes evident at the same time, however, the exposition of this chapter does not seem to verify the preface's clear cut dichotomy between pre-expressive silence and dependent sign. Indeed, having stated that the analysis finally surpasses the paradigm of classical epistemology, the subject-object dichotomy, Merleau-Ponty states, "The recognition of speech (*parole*) as an original region (*region originale*) comes naturally late" (Ph.P: 174/303).

Intellectualism and empiricism are both refuted here in the recognition that "the word has a meaning" reducible neither to a chain of external attachments or referents nor to the constitutive intentions of a thought already in possession of itself. In this sense the sign's "dependence" has been revoked. What is originary is not all indebted to the purely non-linguistic. Expression does not just represent an order complete in itself.

> The process of expression, when it is successful, does not merely leave for the reader and the writer a kind of reminder, it brings the signification into existence at the very heart of the text, it brings it to life in an organism of words, establishing it in the writer or the reader as a new sense organ, opening a field or a new dimension to our experience. (Ph.P. 182/212-213).

The act of linguistic expression is not therefore the reappearance in a new guise of an already existent or founded meaning. Rather, with it there is the emergence of a new dimension surpassing both the creative intention of its author and the expectation of the reader. In this sense the process of expression "confers on what it expresses an existence in itself (*en soi*)" (Ph.P: 183/213), one whose modality cannot be subsumed, it seems, under the category of 'dependence' which underwrites the preface. Indeed, as Merleau-Ponty had said straightforwardly earlier in the analysis of the incarnate subject, "repeating" and at the same time altering the formula of the preface, "The relation of expression to expresses or of sign to signification is not a one-way relation (*un rapport à sens unique*) like that which exists between original text and translation" (Ph.P: 166/194).

As a corallary to this recognition of the 'originary' dimension of expression, Merleau-Ponty invokes a radical deconstruction of the classical model of the subject conferring an inner meaning on an external sign, i.e. 'translating' the original, silent, pre-linguistic stratum into a conventional system of signs, its representation.

> Thought is no 'internal' thing and does not exist independently of the world and words. What misleads us in this connection and causes us to believe in a thought which exists for itself prior to expression, is thought already constituted and expressed, which we can silently recall to ourselves, and through which we acquire the illusion of an inner life. But in reality this supposed silence is alive with words, this inner life is an inner language. (Ph.P: 183)

In this perspective it can be seen that an inner content or thought does not stand 'behind' the sign. Rather, "thought and expression are simultaneously constituted" within the *institution* of speech. And *vis à vis* this event the attributes comprising the classical notion of the *subject*, the inner versus the outer, the active versus the passive, etc. are seen to fail.

> Language certainly has an interior, but this is not self-subsistent and self-conscious thought. What does language express, if it does not express thoughts? It presents or rather it is the subject's taking up of a position in the world of his significations. (Ph.P: 193)

If "expression" (a term Merleau-Ponty never disregards) is not a matter of a one-way conferral between two parallel strata, if the linguistic dimension is not just a repetition of a more original domain, then thought cannot be 'inside' creating the sign. Rather speech and thought are enveloped in one another and thought tends toward the sign as towards it completion. In the discursive event neither term, neither thought nor its sign can be classified as active and made responsible for the resulting content. Creative intentions are "instituted"—they arise here only on the basis of a certain passivity: "the new significative intention knows itself only in recovering itself from already available significations, the result of prior acts of expression" (Ph.P: 183/213). The analysis of the speech act therefore anticipates the 'centrifugal/centripetal' dialectic that emerges in the closing chapter on freedom.[8] And just as there the analysis of 'situated freedom' displaces the classical notions of will, subjectivity, and *Sinngebung*, so here the classical subject has become a speaking subject and it no longer arrives at the sign with a text ready to translate into knowledge. Later in the article, "Indirect Language and the Voices of Silence," which, as Lefort notes,[9] is the first place that Merleau-Ponty's full break with classical metaphysics and the philosophy of consciousness occurs, perhaps the full effect of the analyses of the body as expression and speech begin to be felt:

> Expressive speech does not simply choose a sign for an already defined signification, as one goes to look for a hammer in order to drive a nail or for a claw to pull it out. It gropes around a significative intention which is not guided by any text, and which is precisely in the process of writing the text. (Signs: 46)

To grasp the significance of this recognition and the revision it will force, however, it will be necessary to return to the other side of the *Phenomenology's* account of language.

III.

The question of language is taken up in detail in the *Phenomenology* also in its discussion of the Cogito (part three, chapter one). Here the thematic return upon the considerations and perspective that the preface *re*writes.

> The *Cogito* is either this thought which took shape three centuries ago in the mind of Descartes, or the meaning (*sens*) of the books he has left for us, or else an eternal truth which emerges from them, but in any case is a cultural being of which it is true to say that my thought strains towards it rather than that it embraces it, as my body, in familiar surroundings finds its orientation and makes its way among objects without my needing to have them expressly in mind. (Ph.P: 369)

But how is it that, in any case, the *Cogito* is a cultural being? And, how is it connected with language, that entity by means of which, as he notes, consciousness is engaged in history (Ph.P: 399)?

In this chapter Merleau-Ponty argues that behind all our particular thoughts, words, or percepts, there must remain "a retreat (*reduit*) of non-being, a self" (Ph.P: 400). In reading Descartes' *Meditations* one comes across an empirical and statistical meaning of the words '*sum*' and '*Cogito*,' but these signs would be without any sense, not even an inauthentic one, were I not before the emergence of the discursive event already in contact with an anterior realm of significance at the level of the lived. Words at the empirical and statistical level can be meaningful, then, only if there is an originary dimension which gives rise to them. This dimension must be in the strictest sense, speechless.

One can distinguish then a *Cogito* which is arrived at by *reading* Descartes, i.e. one grasped "only through the medium of language." This spoken Cogito (*Cogito parlé*) is first described in more literal terms in the *Phenomenology* as a "Cogito over (*sur*) language" (Ph.P: 400/459), one which remains trapped in the expressive medium. At this level one remains stuck in the idea, rather than actually practicing the Cogito. One is involved with 'immortalizing' a truth which constantly escapes, "fixing our life in conceptual forms" (Ph.P: 402)—a point from which he interprets the abstracted essences of Husserl which belong, as the preface notes, to the derivations of linguistic forms.

The Cogito which appears only through the medium of language does not, however, have "existence in itself," to use his earlier qualifier. It stands at a level which remains dependent and even this qualifier does not go far enough as a characterization of signs.

> I should find them not so much *derivative* and inauthentic as *meaningless*, and I should be unable to even read Descartes' book, were I not, before any speech can begin in contact with my own life and thought, and if the spoken cogito did not encounter within me a tacit Cogito (*cogito tacite*). (Ph.P: 402; my emphasis).

If the 'higher' Cogito were first characterized as a 'Cogito over language' this more original level and its flux is to be seen as the "silent Cogito (*Cogito silencieux*) . . . the one Descartes sought when writing his *Meditations*" and as "the condition of the read Cogito (*Cogito lu*)" (Ph.P: 402/460). And just as the search for the Cogito in the Second Meditation admonishes us to elevate "ourselves above the dubitable forms of locution that the vulgar invent" (*ex formis loquendi quas vulgus dubitationem quaesivisse*),[10] so here too we are displaced beyond the false confines of language; this time to the primordial silence standing behind it. It is this level which both funds and incites the expressive act. "Descartes would not even have tried to put these expressive operations into operation had he not in the first place caught a glimpse (*un vue*) of his existence" (Ph.P: 402). The relation which makes language possible then is a relation of grounds, of *fundierung*, of a *conditio sine qua non*. Merleau-Ponty's argument here is based upon the necessity of an original 'text' for all signs to refer back to, the necessity of a "pre-text" which would unconditionally account for all meaning and would be itself unconditioned. In this regard the *Phenomenology* remains a thoroughly classical work and might be easily aligned with the position of Sartre at the time:

> It doesn't matter what Descartes *says* of the *Cogito*. What counts is that when I understand a word, I must evidently be conscious of understanding it . . . . But when I am conscious of understanding a word, no word is interpolated between me and myself. The word, the single word in question, is there before (*devant*) me, as that which is understood.[11]

Nonetheless, despite the classical and even Cartesian leanings of the *Phenomenology*, it would be falsifying not to recognize its attempt to broaden this foundational approach to the interface between language and the perceived world. Precisely against the view of Sartre against

Parain that has been noted, grounding the sign in the objectivating syntheses of identification and the regard of consciousness, Merleau-Ponty argues that the word does *not* just exist *before* consciousness. Sartre had said that what makes the word 'sleet,' for example, identical and meaningful throughout its various instantiations was the foundation that consciousness alone can provide. And this in turn rests upon the specificity of the silent presence to self that such a consciousness implies: I know what I want to express, because I know it "without intermediary."[12] It is then to consciousness that Sartre turns in answering the following question: "I now ask Parain where is the *word* 'sleet' (*gresil*), that non-temporal and non-extended reality that is both on the page of the book, in the vibration in the air, in that moist mouthful I swallow and that does not let itself be absorbed by any of these particular phenomena?"[13]

In taking up a position on these polemics, Merleau-Ponty shows he can side comfortably with neither side:

> Am I to say that the word 'sleet' is the unified idea of these manifestations, and that it exists only for my consciousness and through a synthesis of identification? To do so would be to forget what psychology has taught us about language. To speak, as we have seen, is not to call up verbal images and articulate words in accordance with the imagined model. By undertaking a critical examination of the verbal image, and showing that the speaking subject plunges into speech without imagining the words he is about to utter, modern psychology eliminates the word as representation or as an object for consciousness and reveals a motor presence of the word which is not the knowledge of the word. The word 'sleet,' when it is known to me is not an object which I recognize through any identificatory synthesis, but a certain use made my phonatory equipment, a certain modulation of my body as a being in the world. Its generality is not that of an idea but that of a behavioral style.
>
> (Ph.P: 403)

The analysis of the incarnate subject undertaken in the *Phenomenology* thus in a sense already involves its author in the attempt to transcend what it had called "philosophies of consciousness" (Ph.P: 168). Further, one can see to what extent Merleau-Ponty's 'expectation' that Sartre should "elaborate a theory of passivity" in an article published the same year as the *Phenomenology* was already itself a criticism (S.N.S.: 77). With regard to the problem of language this means, Merleau-Ponty holds, it must be recognized that the meaningful character of the sign is not constituted by the inner conferring acts of self-conscious thought. It occurs by the sign's being "seized and assumed" within the phonemic producing powers of the subject and the particular expressive possibilities which the system of signs offers it. In both cases the totalitizing project of consciousness is decentered.

In this regard it can be noted that while, as will be seen, Merleau-Ponty increasingly moves towards the view of language as an irreducible originary element and less and less the contrary of a primordial silence that it is to represent, Sartre holds on to the 'Cartesian' grids of the earlier position that grounded the sign in an objectifying *gaze*, i.e. in its standing *before* consciousness. In an interview published in 1965 and reprinted in *Situations IX*, he states:

> (F)or me the signified is the object. I will define my language which is not necessarily that of the linguists. This chair is the object, it is therefore the signified. Then there is the signification, the logical totality which will be constituted by words, the signification of a sentence. If I say, "This table is in front of the window," I intend a signified, which is the table, with the significations, which is the sentential totality (*l'ensemble des phrases*) that is constituted. And I consider myself as the signifier (*significant*). The signification is the noema, the correlate of the totality of vocal elements pronounced.[14]

The discursive event then can be explained again along classical lines. "The articulation of the signifiers gives (*donne*) the signification which in its turn intends the signified . . . "[15] Nonetheless, Sartre is aware that this donation, this *Sinngebung*, is never more than partial. Indeed it is in a sense perpetually undone, since "I utilize words which have themselves a history and a relation to the totality of language."[16] The content of the sign, however, could be reducible to the purity of a conscious regard only if the sign did not have its own history, only if it did not have its own role and value within the play of signs—only if, in short, to use Satre's own words, linguistic creativity, the creative transformations of the subject, were in fact truly creative, and not "always a secondary fact" dependent upon the specific make-up of a linguistic practice for its intelligibility.

IV.

Merleau-Ponty's Cartesianism, even in the *Phenomenology* is a modified one, then. In effect, we are to look beneath the sign *and* beneath consciousness to its belonging—to the lived body and its Being-in-the-world. But the extent to which this position still remains a "philosophy of consciousness" can be measured in the conclusion Merleau-Ponty draws from his considerations on the Cogito and the issues which provoked Sartre's reply to Parain. Having emphasized the role of the body in this discussion, he concludes:

> Thus language presupposes nothing less than a con-sciousness of language, a silence of consciousness which envelops the speaking world (*monde parlant*) and where words first receive configuration and sense (*sens*). That is why consciousness is never subordinated to any empirical language, why languages can be translated and learned, and finally, why language is not an attribute of external origin, in the sociologist's sense. Behind the spoken cogito, the one that is converted into discourse and into essential truth, there lies a tacit cogito, a proof (*epreuve*) of self by self. (Ph.P: 403/462)

The first thing to notice here is that despite the *decentrement* which the analysis of the body has effected, this conclusion is proferred in terms of the necessities and the order of consciousness, "the presence of self to self" which is, he states, "existence itself" (Ph.P: 404/462). That is, the silence which the sign presupposes is not posited in terms of a silence of the body, but one of consciousness. Secondly, this conclusion still holds that whatever it is that is transcendental about language must be grasped *outside* it, or more properly, 'beneath it.' Empirical languages are not to be explained away in some form of transcendental language, a *language sauvage* which would itself account for the question of origins (in this regard, the *texte originale* of the preface remains metaphorical, it is again more precisely the "pre-text") or even an experience which would be 'linguistic' in some manner. It is only silence which explains Sartre's "vibration of the air" and this silence is the latter's opposite. Finally, as a corollary to this, the thrust of these analyses, for reasons that have already become clear, cannot but call into question the analyses in the chapter on expression where the sign's existence *en soi* was disclosed—as opposed to the 'essentialist' tendencies here in which the sign 'immortalizes' and reproduces the kernal of the *significatum*.

Nonetheless, if this foundation and its priority is established, the silence of consciousness has not thereby been proven to be independent of its expression, a matter which adds an element of ambiguity to the order established with the tacit Cogito. In a vestage of the disclosure of the incompleteness of thought prior to language in the chapter on expression and speech, Merleau-Ponty adds that the tacit Cogito remains incomplete apart from language.

> The consciousness which conditions language is merely a comprehensive and inarticulate grasp of the world, like that of the infant at its first breath or of the man who is about to drown and is thrown (*se rue*) toward life, and if it is true that any particular knowledge is founded (*fonde*) on this primary view (*vue*), it is also true that it awaits to be reconquered, fixed, and explicated by perceptual exploration and speech. (Ph.P: 404/463).

Language is conditioned by consciousness. But this consciousness is a particular kind—not reflective but perceptual consciousness. The inarticulate grasp which *founds* language is a primordial *view* which awaits explication and further clarification. That is, ". . . this original text is perception itself" (Ph.P: 21). It is this which lies beneath language, rendering it meaningful. At the same time, however, the *founding* term here is *incomplete*: it itself only becomes realized in the *founded*, in expression. "The tacit Cogito is a Cogito only when it has found expression for itself" (Ph.P: 404)—only when it has become that derivative and dependent Cogito it was invoked to explain and which remained meaningless without it. It is the ambiguity of this 'belonging-together' the circling back of founding and founded terms in the relation between language and perception which forms the limits of the account in the *Phenomenology*.

V.

The working notes to *The Visible and the Invisible* reopen the question of this belonging-together within the framework of a renewed call for an *Ursprungsklärung*. This *Ursprungsklärung* involves a radicalization of the standpoint of the *Phenomenology of Perception* through moving beyond the 'consciousness/object' distinction which centers it (V.I.: 200). And, this radicalization is not without its effect on the position on the status of language relative to perception developed in the earlier work.

The criticism of the *Phenomenology* is evident as early as the opening published notes from early 1959. In a note from February of that year entitled 'Tacit Cogito and Speaking Subject' Merleau-Ponty delineates the tension in the *Phenomenology* that has been followed out here. Engaged in the task of discovering an intersubjectivity which is not perspectival (i.e. based on a gaze), but 'vertical,' he states:

> The tacit Cogito does not of course, solve these problems. In disclosing it as I did in Ph.P. I did not arrive at a solution (my chapter on the Cogito is not connected with the chapter on speech): on the contrary I posed a problem. The tacit Cogito should make understood how language is not impossible, but cannot make understood how it is possible. (V.I.: 175-6)

What does this enigmatic statement involve? Well, first of all it cannot mean, as has been seen, that the chapter on the Cogito had nothing to say about speech—that considerations on the Cogito had not touched the thematics of speech. Indeed, if anything, it is precisely its preoccupation with speech that led to the explicit reasoning and formulation that resulted in the doctrine of the tacit Cogito. In another note to *The Visible and the Invisible*, Merleau-Ponty recounts this reasoning, explicating its concern with signification and expression. Likewise, it should be noted, its connection with Sartre is not left silent. He states:

> The Cogito of Descartes (reflection) is an operation over (*sur*) significations, a statement of relations between them (and the significations themselves sedimented in acts of expression). It therefore presupposes a prereflective contact of self with self (the non-thetic consciousness [of] self Sartre) or a tacit Cogito (being close by oneself)—this is how I reasoned in Ph.P. (V.I.: 170-171/ 224)

The fact that the two chapters within the *Phenomenology* are unconnected must be explained on other than thematic grounds. Rather, what needs to be explained is all that the considerations on the Cogito left *unthought* concerning the originary and expression—and consequently what does not fall within the order that the tacit Cogito founds.

In presenting an argument for a *conditio sine qua non* here, a "ground of which one could not say anything" (V.I.: 175), but from which everything might be said, the doctrine of the tacit Cogito may have satisfied the 'positivistic' demand that needs the reassurance that speech is not impossible, but it does not tell us anything about how it is so. Rather, it simply tells how consciousness remains indecinable. And this means, to return to Merleau-Ponty's criticism of the doctrine, that "there remains the problem of the passage from the perceptual meaning (*sens*) to the language meaning, from behavior to thematization" (V.I.: 176). That is, there remains still to be grasped the specificity of their relation, one still described here as a 'passage.'

But that is not all that is problematic about the doctrine. For this argument to reach a *positive* foundation in the silence of consciousness, a certain abstraction, perhaps even a *transcendental illusion* must be involved. Referring to the reasoning behind the tacit Cogito outlined above, he states:

> Is this correct? What I call the tacit Cogito is impossible. To have the idea of "thinking" (in the sense of the "thought of seeing and of feeling"), to make the reduction, to return to immanence and to the consciousness of . . . it is necessary to have words. It is by combination of words (with their charge of sedimented significations, which are in principle capable of entering into other relations than the relations that have served to form them) that I *form* the transcendental attitude, that I *constitute* the constitutive consciousness. The words do not refer to positive significations and finally to the flux of the *Erlebnisse* as *Selbstgegeben*. Mythology of a self-consciousness to which the word "consciousness" would refer—There are only differences between significations. (V.I.: 171)

The argument for the tacit Cogito invokes a mythology. Words do not refer to individual significations and finally to a foundation in the presence to self of the lived. The hierarchial structure that facilitated the myth of silent self-consciousness must then be displaced. The immanence of the silent Cogito, this direct contact of self by self is not untouched by the medium and its charge of sedimented significations that by itself (i.e. as a *Cogito parlé*), was taken to be meaningless. The distinction, the separation between language and the silent or nonlinguistic stratum or layer cannot be absolute.

Likewise, then, he will have to give up the ideal of a transparent medium which would simply reduplicate the realm of silence, if there is no means of direct access to the latter. In a note discussing the return to what he calls the originary or 'savage' being, he states:

> But I will then have to disclose a non-explicated horizon: that of the language I am using to describe all that—And which codetermines its final meaning.

> Therefore, very important, from the introduction on to introduce the problem of the tacit Cogito and the language Cogito. Naiveté of Descartes who does not see a tacit cogito under the language of *Wesen*, of significations—But Naiveté also of a silent Cogito that would deem itself to be an adequation with the silent consciousness, whereas its very description of silence rests entirely on the virtues of language. (V.I.: 179-80)

These texts seem to point, however, to a certain scepticism or entrapment of the speaker in the linguistic system. If language is always already a horizon behind the grasp of the signified, how will the "return to the things themselves" which prompts phenomenology ever be accomplished? Would not the result be, to use a phrase of Foucault, "*language a l'infini?*"

Yet this is not the point of Merleau-Ponty's recognition—not that he is unaware of the difficulty involved:

> If we dream of finding again the natural world or time through coincidence, of being identical to the O-point which we see yonder, or to the pure memory which from the depths of ourselves governs our acts of recall, then language is a power for error, since it cuts the continuous tissue that joins us vitally to the things and to the past and is installed between ourselves and that tissue like a screen. (V.I.: 125)

So long as one holds that language remains only the translation of an original text, and that this translation can be readily had through a fusion between consciousness and the perceived world, then these considerations are not a problem. But if, on the contrary, it is recognized that there is no direct access to the given and if, therefore, we cannot claim that thought univocally conditions language—but that it itself does not go unconditioned—then language ceases to appear as the mirror-image and the self-effacing re-presentation of the given and the 'translation' involved takes on an uneffaceable undecidability. In this light the sign is not reducible without remainder.

Having recognized this irreducibility, however, Merleau-Ponty does not foreclose the attempt to "return to the things themselves." Recognizing what he has called the "mythology" behind the tacit Cogito and its direct contacts with self and the world, he states in the note on the tacit Cogito from Jan., 1959: "Yet there is a world of silence, the perceived world at least is an order where there are non-language significations—yes non-language significations, but they are not accordingly *positive"* (V.I.: 171). The return to this original 'silence' cannot be based on a grid of positive terms; it is not the return to a *tabula rasa*. There are no positivities apart from our grasp and the horizon of its occurence. In this sense the things of the perceived world arise diacritically within a network of divergences. That is, the terms of the perceived world are to be understood just as speech is in terms of the differentiation of a field, a conception Merleau-Ponty had discovered through the examination of Saussure.

> The Saussurian analysis of the relations between signifiers and the relations from signifier to signified and between the significations (as differences between significations) confirms and rediscovers the idea of perception as *divergence (écart)* by relation to a level, that is, the idea of the primordial Being, of the Convention of conventions, of the speech before speech. (V.I.: 201)[17]

This however dictates a new understanding of the *Ineinander* character of language and perception:

> . . . . for there is no hierarchy of orders or layers or planes (always founded on the individual-essence distinction), there is dimensionality of every fact and facticity of every dimension—This in virtue of the "ontological difference— (V.I.: 270)

As has been seen, however, it is precisely this individual/essence paradigm, with its accompanying hierarchy of orders and planes—implying an opposition between language and silence, sign and signified, object and subject (and the dependency of the first of these couplets on the second)—that has structured the doctrine of the *Cogito tacite*. In invoking Heidegger's 'ontological difference' here Merleau-Ponty has attempted to surmount the failures of his earlier classicism and the metaphysical order which structured it.

IV.

In *The Origin of the Work of Art*, among other places, Heidegger himself takes up the question of the specificity of the belonging-together of perception and language, asking whether the latter en-frames our 'conception' of things or vice versa. In the case at hand, he concerns himself with asking in particular whether the medieval conception of thingness as substance with its accidents is derived from theory of the predicative judgement:

> Is the structure of a simple propositional statement (the combination of subject and predicate) the mirror image of the structure of the thing (of the union of substance and accidents)? Or could it be that even the structure of the thing as thus envisaged is a projection of the framework of the sentence?
>
> What could be more obvious than that man transposes his propositional way of understanding things into the structure of the thing itself? Yet this view, seemingly critical yet actually rash and ill-considered, would have to explain how such a transposition of propositional structure is supposed to be possible without the thing having already become visible.[18]

The first question here is doubtless the matter which lies at the center of the problematic concerning the tacit cogito and its 'overcoming' in *The Visible and the Invisible*: the question of the specificity of the belonging-together of language and perception. The second, that man transposes his propositional structure or linguistic grid to the thing is the stance of several schools in twentieth century thought: it has been raised here in Parain's name, the position that Sartre and the early Merleau-Ponty are posited against. Finally, the answer to this second question, that it must explain the *possibility* of such a transposition or imposition of the sign on the thing without the first becoming visible, is the answer of classical phenomenology—and has been seen to stand behind Sartre's view as well as the argument for the *Cogito tacite* in the *Phenomenology*.

Heidegger, however, is satisfied with neither thesis: rather, it is precisely this classically founded investigation which fails to provide us with an easy answer:

> The question which comes first and functions as the standard, proposition structure or thing-structure remains to this hour undecided. It remains even doubtful whether in this form the question is at all decidable.[19]

Invoking Merleau-Ponty's similar considerations on the tacit Cogito it can be added—How in fact could it be *decidable* in this form? Could Sartre ever convince us that this infrasilence he *describes*—for which he posts a sign—is with regard to language totally unconditioned? On the other hand, how could it be the case that Being could be reducible to a sign—that instead of the sign's dependence on the signified there might be an inversion making Being dependent upon the sign—since inherent to the very structure of the sign is its being a sign *of*?[20] How could the signified be simply reducible to a sign?

Heidegger's own adjudication over this antinomy is the following:

> Actually, the sentence structure does not provide the standard for the pattern of the thing-structure, nor is the latter simply mirrored in the former. Both sentence and thing structure derive, in their typcial form and their possible mutual relationship from a common and more original source.[21]

In this sense there could be no question of priority between sign and signified, ground and grounded, designatum and description. The manner in which words and things belong-together would no longer be thinkable in terms of these simple oppositions, but rather would need to be grasped in terms of their mutual implication in the appropriation of the significative event itself, in the difference and chiasm which marks the emergence of each. Hence, Merleau-Ponty similarly states in a note on 'the world' (Dec., 1959):

> Replace the notions of concept, idea, mind, representation with the notions of dimensions, articulation, level, hinges, pivots, configuration—The point of departure = the critique of the usual conception of the *thing* and its *properties* logical inherence critique of the positive signification (differences between significations), signification as a separation (*écart*), theory of prediction—founded on this diacritical conceptio. (V.I.: 224)

VII.

Yet, as has been seen, the task of exploring an originary 'silence' is not done away with in *The Visible and the Invisible*. It does, however, undergo a certain shift and here the distance between it and the classical leanings of the earlier work becomes definitive. First, it has become evident that this 'silence' of the transcendental domain is no longer available as an immediate or positive term, as the doctrine of the Cogito necessitated. Nor can the distinction between the linguistic, the sounded, and the silent, the "transcendental field" of the perceived world, as he once called it (Ph.P:61), be simply a matter of *opposi-*

tion. Rather, it would be necessary to recognize the involvement of language in that field, And, if the question of the 'transcendental' or the 'originary' is still to be thought of in terms of 'silence' it would be necessary to see how the latter overdetermines language as well, a move Merleau-Ponty undertakes in asserting that "there would be needed a silence that envelops speech anew . . . (and) this silence will not be the contrary of language" (V.I.: 179).

What sort of chiasm does this imply, though? In one of the final notes to this work (Nov., 1960) Merleau-Ponty relates what he has in mind.

> Silence of perception = the object made of wires of which I could not say what it is, nor how many sides it has, etc. and which nonetheless is there.
> There is an analogous *silence of language* i.e. a language that no more involves *acts of reactivated signification* than does this perception—and which nonetheless functions and *inventively* it is it that is involved in the fabrication of a book. (V.I.: 268—my emphasis)

Language would then be seen to have a certain 'silence' as well. The sign would not simply involve an event of reactivated signification. No more than the transcendence of the perceived object could its Being be exhausted in a constitutive act or *Sinngebung*; it could not be reduced to what Sartre had called its standing *before* consciousness. It would be, in other words, itself originary. But this is to say just what Merleau-Ponty had held in the chapter on expression and speech and which was *excluded* from the doctrine of the Cogito in the *Phenomenology*.

In fact, for reasons which have become clear now, the doctrine of the tacit Cogito *had* to make this exclusion, based as it was on what he called the individual/essence distinction and a strategy of significative 'layers.' But if the sign itself has "an analogous silence" to it comparable to that of the originality of the perceptual field, it must be irreducible to the significative reactivation of a content that is to be found on an existential level more primordially elsewhere. In this sense the separation which Merleau-Ponty refers to in his criticism of the *Cogito tacite* divides the *Phenomenology of Perception* against itself. The full recognition of the contradiction would only come after a prolonged investigation that placed language and expression at its center. Still, one can note again the extent to which the elements for the surpassing it implicated are already gathered in the 1952 article whose decisive status Lefort has pointed out:

Now if we rid our minds of the idea that our language is the translation or cipher of an original text, we shall see that the idea of a complete expression is nonsensical, and that all language is indirect or allusive—that it is, if you wish, silence. (Signs: 43)

VIII.

What Merleau-Ponty had discovered about the sign would not fit then into the classical framework by which he and his phenomenological progenitors had understood the Cogito. That is, . . ."it would be naive to seek solidity in a heaven of ideas or in a *ground* of meaning *(fond du sens)*" (V.I.: 116). But if the content involved here is originary, is not reducible to a ground beneath it, then the problematic of *Ursprungsklärung* with respect to it has been transformed. As he put it elsewhere in the text of *The Visible and the Invisible*:

The originary *(originaire)* is not of one sole type, it is not all behind us; the restoration of the true past, of the pre-existence is not all of philosophy, the lived experience is not flat, without depth, without dimension, it is not an opaque stratum with which we have to merge. The appeal to the originary goes in several directions; the originary breaks up *(éclate)*, and philosophy must accompany this break up, this non-coincidence, this differentiation. (V.I.: 124/165).

With the recognition of this 'break-up' of the originary and the attempt to arrive at, to 'merge' with an absolute ground or 'stratum' to which all things might be referred, the sign can no longer be thought significant *due* to what stands behind or beneath it. It cannot be held to be the mere re-presentation of a stratum from which, on the contrary, it marks a divergence, *un écart*. Conversely, the visible cannot be a realm complete in itself, the original that all 'ideality' would only attempt to capture, as had been required in the classical reading of the earlier work.[22]

In this regard, if, for example, the claim of Gérard Granel that Merleau-Ponty's later work involves an "agonizing reappraisal"[23] of the *Phenomenology of Perception* and classical phenomenology in general is overblown, certainly the foundation awarded perception as the "infrastructure" over *(sur)* which the superstructures constructed by intelligence are "established" (Ph.P.: 53) has been, to use an Hegelian notion, 'dispersed' *(zerstreut)*. In fact, as Geraets has noticed[24] the deconstruction undertaken by Merleau-Ponty's later work concentrates now on an overdetermined notion of *"la foi perceptive."* As the latter states:

> For us, the "perceptual faith" includes everything that is given to the natural man in the original in an experience source, with the force of what is inaugural and present in person, according to a view that for him is ultimate and could not conceivably be more perfect or closer—whether we are considering things perceived in the ordinary sense of the word, or his initiation into the past, the imaginary, language, the predicative truth of science, works of art, the others, or history. (V.I.: 158)

Again, however, it is not the case that this recognition was absent from the *Phenomenology*. There, too, Merleau-Ponty spoke of a narrow sense of 'perception' and a wider sense, one which involves *"connaissance des existences"* (Ph.P.: 40/50). In contradistinction to the later work, however, the *Phenomenology* could not just speak of perception as a simple model or "archetype" (V.I.: 158). It was framed in the *metaphysical* categories which have been followed out here in relation to language, i.e. in this framework perception is more than an 'archetype,' it is a layer of significance which is foundational and ultimate, one in relation to which all others become significant.

Seen in this light it is metaphysics which separates the *Phenomenology of Perception* from the direction taken by *The Visible and the Invisible*, not simply a move from phenomenology to ontology as is sometimes claimed. In fact, as is evident, the earlier work was equally 'ontological.' Rather, this move is one from a metaphysical model (or perhaps 'Metaphysics' itself) to its other, from what Merleau-Ponty refers to in his later works as a horizontal to a vertical model, or perhaps from "Being" to what Marc Richir has called its "ruins."[25] In the fracture of this horizontal conception encased in the categories of complete presence and dependence, ground and grounded, essence and existence, a new conception of the problematic that has been followed out here emerges, this time at the limits of *The Visible and the Invisible*—and it might be said that it involves the heart of the task which it laid out for itself, reinstating the issue that was this project's catalyst immediately following the *Phenomenology's* publication.[26] In the final paragraph of the prepared text, returning to this issue, Merleau-Ponty states:

> We shall have to follow more closely this transition from

the mute world to the speaking world. For the moment we want to suggest that one can speak neither of a destruction nor of a construction of silence (and still less of a destruction that conserves or of a radicalization that destroys—which is not to solve but to pose the problem). When the silent vision falls into speech, and when the speech in turn, opening up the field of the nameable and the sayable, inscribes itself in that field, in its place, according to its truth—in short when it metamorphoses the structures of the visible world and makes itself a gaze of the mind, *intuitus mentis*—this is always in virtue of the same fundamental phenomenon of reversibility which sustains both the mute perception and the speech and which manifests itself by an almost carnal existence of the idea, as well as by a sublimation of the flesh. (V.I.: 154-5).

This fundamental phenomenon of reversibility, this chiasm which leaves neither element unchanged, is precisely what forced the recognition that language could no longer be understood as a feature merely added on to perception. Perception could no longer be seen as the text which provides the lexicon for all others. In fact there never was such a text—no visible which could be isolated from its invisible, no signified that could appear apart from its sign. Language could not, consequently, as the *Phenomenology* held, be simply established on a perceptual infrastructure. Rather, as he was to say of thought which in turn belongs itself to language, "it must be brought to appear (*la faire apparaître*) directly in (*dans*) the infrastructure of vision" (V.I.: 145). Merleau-Ponty chooses his words carefully at this point, fully cognizant of the overthrow that has been carried out. He states immediately, "brought to appear, we say, and not brought to birth (*la faire nâitre*).

In the absence of this immediate layer of signification, the *Phenomenology's* 'pre-text,' the origin in which it was inscribed breaks up. It can no longer, then, be a question of unearthing the primordial view by which the self is in contact with itself and its world, "the unique structure which is *presence*" (Ph.P.: 430/492). Rather, if the problematic of *Ursprungsklärung* and the search for the transcendental moment it implies is to be retained, it will be necessary to recognize just how difficult that investigation becomes outside its classical grids.

This is a difficulty which the latter work of Merleau-Ponty continually reaffirms. To accomplish its goal it necessitated dislodging the analysis of what it called our opening unto Being from the metaphysics of the Cogito—either at the 'level' of thought, or by moving underground to the level of the 'lived.' For this underground, as the development of Merleau-Ponty's work demonstrates, is no more a fixed point than any other of the grounds of classical thought. Rather than the fulfillment of the Cogito, the notion of the lived led to the recognition of its exhaustion. And, it necessitated an understanding of both language *and* perception outside the classical accounts.

In a discussion in "Eye and Mind" which returns, as had *The Structure of Behavior* over two decades before it to a consideration of Descartes' *Dioptrique*, Merleau-Ponty states:

> Now perhaps we have a better sense of what is meant by that little verb "to see." Vision is not a certain mode of thought or presence to self; it is the means given me for being absent from myself, for being present at the fission of Being from inside—the fission at whose termination, and not before, I come back to myself. (Primacy: 186)

NOTES

[1]References in this paper to the texts of Merleau-Ponty are to the standard editions and translations of his works. In cases where minor corrections to the English translations have been made, the English pagination is followed by the French original. Abbreviations are as follows:

Ph.P.	*Phenomenology of Perception.* tr. Colin Smith. New York: Humanities Press, 1962. A translation of *Phenomenologie de la perception.* Paris: Gallimard, 1945.
Primacy:	"Eye and Mind," tr. Carleton Dallery in *The Primacy of Perception* ed. James M. Edie. Evanston: Northwestern University Press, 1964. A translation of "L'Oeil et l'esprit," *Les Temps Modernes,* 17: 184-5, 1961.
Signs	"Indirect Language and the Voices of Silence," tr. Richard C. Mc-Cleary in *Signs.* Evanston: Northwestern University Press. A translation of "Le Language indirect et les voix du silence," *Les Temps Modernes,* 7:80, 8:81, 1952.
S.N.S.	*Sense and Non-Sense* tr. Hubert L. Dreyfus & Patricia L. Dreyfus. Evanston: Northwestern University Press, 1964. A translation of *Sens et non-sens.* Paris: Nagel, 1948.
V.I.	*The Visible and the Invisible.* tr. Alphonso Lingis. Evanston: Northwestern University Press, 1968. A translation of *Le visible et l'invisible.* Paris: Gallimard, 1964.

[2]Jean-Paul Sartre, "Departure and Return" in *Literary and Philosophical Essays,* tr. Annette Michelson. (New York: Collier Books, 1962, p. 149. This is a translation of

"Aller et Retour" which appeared originally in *Cahiers du Sud*, 264, Fev., 1944.

³Edmund Husserl, *Ideas: General Introduction to Pure Phenomenology*, tr. W.R. Boyce Gibson (New York: Humanities Press, 1931), pp. 348-9.

⁴See Brice Parain, *Recherches sur la nature et les fonctions du langage* (Paris: Gallimard, 1942).

⁵Sartre, op. cit., p. 195/216.

⁶Dominick LaCapra, *A Preface to Sartre* (Ithaca: Cornell University Press), p. 26.

⁷Jean-Paul Sartre, *Being and Nothingness* tr. Hazel E. Barnes (New York: Philosophical Library, 1956), p. 354.

⁸See Ph.P., p. 439.

⁹Claude Lefort, "Qu'est-ce Que Voir?" in *Sur une colonne absente: écrits autour de Merleau-Ponty* (Paris: Gallimard, 1978), p. 153.

¹⁰René Descartes, *Meditations De Prima Philosophia* (Paris: Vrin, 1978), p. 32.

¹¹Sartre, "Departure and Return," p. 171.

¹²ibid, p. 172.

¹³ibid, p. 169.

¹⁴Jean-Paul Sartre, "L'Ecrivain Et Sa Langue" in *Situations IX* (Paris: Gallimard, 1972), pp. 47-48. For further discussion of this text, see Hugh J. Silverman, "Sartre And Structuralism," *International Philosophical Quarterly*, Vol. XVIII, No. 3, p. 342.

¹⁵ibid.

¹⁶ibid.

¹⁷Merleau-Ponty's use of Saussurian linguistics has been explicated in a paper presented by me at the 1977 meeting of the Merleau-Ponty Circle, "Merleau-Ponty's Involvement with Saussure," and is expected to appear shortly.

¹⁸Martin Heidegger, "The Origin of the Work of Art" in *Poetry, Langauge, Thought* tr. Albert Hofstadter (New York: Harper & Row, 1971), p. 24.

¹⁹ibid.

²⁰cp. Jacques Derrida's assertion that "(t)he signifier will never by rights precede the signified in which case it would no longer be a signifier and the 'signifying' signifier would no longer have a possible signified." *Of Grammatology* tr. Gayatri Chakravorty Spivak (Baltimore: Johns Hopkins University Press, 1976), p. 324n.

²¹Heidegger, op. cit.

²²In notes taken by George Klein at Merleau-Ponty's Feb., 1955 Collège de France lectures on The Problem of Passivity, a similar recognition can be found:

> In my book on the phenomenology of perception I underestimated the richness and complexity of the perceived world. I paid too much attention to the perception of mere things, and thus did not devote enough attention to the gaps and incompleteness in our perception . . . . Our perception is mostly of symbols, vectoral, full of question and exclamation marks. *Dingwahrnehmung* is a function of culture, including philosophical culture.

It is about this same time that Merleau-Ponty's published works begin to develop the theme of "*le intermonde*," the world of institutions, of history, and symbolism: in short a "symbolic space" which is taken up, again, in opposition to the strict subject/object dichotomy that he finds in Sartre. See Merleau-Ponty, *The Adventures of the Dialectic* tr. Joseph Bien (Evanston: Northwestern University Press, 1973), p. 200.

²³See Gèrard Granel, *Le sens du temps et de la perception chez E. Husserl* (Paris: Gallimard, 1968), p. 103.

²⁴See Theodore Geraets, "Le Retour À L'Expérience Perceptive Et Le Sens Du Primat De La Perception," *Diologue* Vol. XV, No. 4, Dec., 1976.

[25]See Marc Richir, "La Defenestration," *L'Arc*, No. 46, 1971.

[26]In a footnote to an article dating from 1947 that projects *The Origin of Truth*, the title, among others, given the notes to *The Visible and the Invisible* prior to March, 1959, Merleau-Ponty states:

> It would obviously be in order to give a precise description of the passage of perceptual faith into explicit truth as we encounter it on the level of language. We intend to do so in a work devoted to "The Origin of Truth." (S.N.S.: 94n)

Eye and Mind

MIKEL DUFRENNE
Université de Paris

Eye and Mind is one of the last texts of Merleau-Ponty and perhaps his finest. Sartre wrote of it, "*Eye and Mind* says all, provided one knows how to decipher it" (*Temps modernes*, n° Merleau-Ponty, p. 372). But would I know how to decipher it? Rather than risk such an undertaking, I would like principally to comment on the title itself.

Eye and Mind. One notices immediately that the two words are treated unequally in the text. Eye appears repeatedly in the writings of Merleau-Ponty while mind is rarely mentioned. No doubt this is due to a certain danger in naming it in the manner that delighted philosophers of mind. For the mind is not an organ like the eye, nor is it a substance that can be designated by a substantive. If it is called by name it is for the purpose of designating certain acts characteristic of what *The Structure of Behavior* called the human order. These acts demonstrate a *cogito* which is manifest to itself as that which seeks to be transparent to itself. They are acts in which is consummated (*se consomme*) the separation of subject and object which has already taken shape, but is not yet completed in vision. In short: thinking as opposed to seeing. My first point of questioning bears precisely upon this *and*. What does this conjunction signify? It cannot signify a dialectical relation since there are only two terms; unless we adhere, as does Adorno, to a negative dialectic. In this case it would then be a relation of opposition as in being and non-being. But it can also be a relation of priority as in cause and effect, or even a relation of complementarity as in form and content. Obviously, only a reading of the text will permit an answer to this question. And if the text stresses one of these meanings of *and*—i.e. opposition—it persuades us perhaps not to exclude the others.

To begin with, the eye is foremost. It is first in the title because it is first in the becoming of man. Man sees before he thinks and no doubt he arrives at thought because vision incites it, though Merleau-Ponty doesn't follow this advent. But it still remains that seeing is opposed to thinking, and it is precisely toward this theme that analyses are directed. For example, if these analyses invoke painting at great length, it is in order to show that, "We cannot see how a mind would be able to paint." All the difficulty of our undertaking lies here. By hardening the opposition, can we still account for the emergence of thinking as well as for the movement which leads existence to a reflexive life? Between seeing and thinking contemporary philosophy is given a mediation: speaking, the contemporary of seeing. But Merleau-Ponty does not invoke this mediation and it is here that Lyotard, for example, raises his principle objection. For Lyotard, Merleau-Ponty forgets that nothing happens before "entry into language," save the still blind vicissitudes of drives. It is true that Merleau-Ponty does not situate speaking in seeing. His analysis of seeing excludes language in the same way that his analysis of painting excludes discourse—not only that of the expert or semiotician, but also that of the painting itself. "Read the story and the painting," Poussin wrote to Chanteloup. Merleau-Ponty does not seem interested in paintings that tell a story, unless it is the fundamental story, the very genesis of appearing. Thus speaking neither kindles nor throws light on seeing. On the other hand, perhaps speaking itself can be understood as a type of seeing. Man who speaks (*l'home parlant*) is in language as he is in the world. He harmonizes with its thickness as he does with the flesh of the sensuous. He lives it by inhabiting it. Moreover, speaking can perhaps be equated in a way to seeing for the purpose of disclosing it (*pour le dire*). Such would be the language of "hyper-reflection" of which *The Visible and the Invisible* speaks. This language "becomes philosophy itself," endeavoring to "express beyond significations our silent contact with things when they are not yet expressed things (*des choses dites*)." Such is indeed the admirable language with which Merleau-Ponty approaches raw being (*l'être brut*), leaving it to be spoken in itself as the dream allows desire to speak.

If philosophy requires this effort, it is because seeing, to repeat, is irreducible to thinking and cannot be understood by it. But what about the reverse? Can we not understand thinking through seeing? Is there not a type of seeing which, far from opposing thinking, would be its auxilliary? When, confronted with a proposition, we say "I see," are we not identifying thought with a type of vision? *Wesenschau* is still *Schau*. Besides, thought has willing recourse to a visible of which it avails itself. One has only to think of geometrical figures, of linguistic trees, or the diagrams of graphic semiology. For Descartes space without hiding places in which these signs are drawn is precisely the in-itself that knowledge masters. We can then ask the following question: Are there not two realms (*régimes*) of vision of which one at least, since it is regulated according to thought, presupposes it; while the other precedes it? Merleau-Ponty does not state this clearly, but it is what Descartes suggests to him. Indeed if we follow Descartes, "There is no vision without thought, but *it is not enough* to think in order to see. Vision . . . is born on occasion from what is happening in the body." It is here that "the enigma of vision is not eliminated by Descartes; it is relegated from the thought of seeing to vision in act" (pp. 210-11). But Descartes is unwilling "to sound out this abyss." What matters to him is the edification of knowledge. Today even science, through metaphysics, dispenses with this deviation.

In face of this renunciation of reflection, one can maintain that Merleau-Ponty directs all his attention to the savage realm (*régime*) of vision, and perhaps all the more so because this realm is never obliterated. For even when the mind inspects signs at its convenience, or as Alan said, when perception puts judgment into play, the eye remains present and open. It remains present and open to the point of sometimes leading astray a well-informed reading, in the same manner that discourse is distorted once figure (*figure*) is introduced into it. Surely what one calls "thought flying over" (*la pensée de survol*) is perhaps the vocation of thinking. It is demonstrated when the subject stands at a distance with respect to the object for the purpose of becoming its "master and possessor." This is precisely the purpose of language when it allows for the passage from presence to representation. However, this thought is never fully realized, as it is always carried by perceptive faith that anchors us in the truth of the sensuous Breton says that eye exists in the savage state, and it may be that it is never completely tamed. It is not tamed when understanding employs it, nor any more when vision, instructed by language, becomes this utilitarian and assuring (*sécuristante*) vision of a prosaic reality.

As for the savage in vision, Merleau-Ponty thinks of it according to the Husserlian model of passive synthesis. This vision does not organize the visible. It does not bestow a meaning upon it, nor does it constitute it as readable and expressible in words (*dicible*). Vision receives the visible, rising from the invisible that still clings to it. One can say at the very most that vision opens itself to the visible which is given to it. This act of giving is an event in the visual field. Lyotard says of this event, "that it cannot be situated anywhere but in the vacant space opened by desire" (*Discours, Figure,* p. 22). He also states that "It belongs to this giving which releases us." But what about this *us*? To think *id*, one must still think *ego*. And why say "release us" rather than "seize us"? We are only released when and because we are seized. If there is an event, something happens to someone. In this case we have an act of giving. It is no doubt correct that the subject doesn't exist prior to the event. He is born with it and from it. A transcendental subject in a transcendental field? Why not. But for Merleau-Ponty this transcendental field is not the place of desire, the ephemeral film across which anonymous fluxes travel. It is raw being, this "originary being," (*originaire*) which the philosopher calls flesh, the "last notion" he says, because it is the first. This event, forever starting anew, which takes place as well as inaugurates place, is the bursting forth of this originary being. Consequently we have the upheaval of appearing. This bursting forth produces a chiasm, and institutes a distance between man and things, born simultaneously and continuing to exist for themselves without ever a radical separation. In addition the reversibility of the visible and the seer (*du visible et du voyant*), this double dehiscence of the visible in the seer and the seer in the visible, attests that "things are secret folds of my flesh" (*Le visible et l' invisible*). Therefore we cannot evade the question of origin. It is not the body which gives access to originary being, it is originary being which gives access to the body. And in the end such is indeed the enigma of vision. Far from the eye explaining vision as a reductive science would want, vision explains the eye. Bergson had already claimed this, but for Merleau-Ponty this resilience (*ressort*) of vision is not creative evolution, it is the bursting forth of originary being.

For the purpose of thinking the unthinkable, Merleau-Ponty examines painting, and in particular the kind of painting that Cézanne established. Classical painting can lead us astray. One is tempted to believe that it originates from and appeals to the mind. On one hand in fact, the painters of the Renaissance lay claim to the promotion of their art to the status of the liberal arts by priding themselves on their use of mathematics in order to substitute an artificial perspective for a natural one. They thus establish drawing on a fundamental law. On the other hand, the viewer they solicit is more concerned with the intelligible than with the sensible. One can see this in the diagrams of Alberti. In order to entertain a painting constructed in this perspective, the viewer has only one eye situated at the required distance, and which is neither spherical nor mobile. But everything changes once painters renounce this exact truth of painting to look for another truth—a primary truth having no need of justification according to the standards of knowledge.

Truth is unveiling. Once again it is the bursting forth of originary being, the "deflagration of being," or the apparition of what Klee calls the *Urbildlich*. This being is not a different agency, even less a transcendental one. It comes into light tearing itself from the invisible at the same moment that vision is awakened. Painting accomplishes what "hyper-reflection" tries to say. What the painter, by dint of patience, wants to see as well as to present for our seeing, is the very birth of seeing in contact with its newly-formed image. He wants to take by surprise this moment when "things become things and world becomes world" (p. 217). He is not interested in what follows, after language or after culture. Nor is he interested in what Adorno calls the administered world where fruit bowls are machine-turned and mountains are explored by geographers. The painter returns to a pre-reality, which is also a sur-reality in the sense meant by the surrealists. Their objective chance is but another name for this inaugural event in which man is still very much mingled with things. The painter leads the noumenon back to what is properly the phenomenon, i.e. to the manifestation of appearing.

One speaks of appearing and not appearance. Cézanne is not an impressionist, even when he invokes "his little sensation." It is not a matter for him of restoring a truth of the seen which would dismiss line while making color vibrate. It is also not a matter of presenting a playing field for phantasms brought about by the deconstruction of a field of representation. Cézanne doesn't deconstruct, he preconstructs. He doesn't break the fruit bowl, he shows us its genesis—not its production, but namely its coming into the visible. This space that the fruit bowl comes to inhabit is not a predetermined space in which it is able to take form. It is a space which springs from it, a dimension of its flesh. And it is definitely a matter of flesh. Flesh is this texture of the sensuous given order here according to the visible. The mathematical logos by which the mind informs reality is unable to account for it, and thus this flesh appeals to another logos, "a system of equivalences, a logos of lines, lights, colors, reliefs, masses (p. 218), according to which a countenance of the world assents to visibility.

Thus the eye deserves to be mentioned first in the title. But is is not for the purpose of designating a determined organ assigned to a precise function, rather it is in order to designate this strange 'power of opening' of flesh. This flesh which is not yet a body, becomes itself reflected once a chiasm is brought about in it. This eye, which puts us into the world by opening a world to us, precedes the mind. But was it still necessary then to mention mind? We know that Merleau-Ponty challenges 'thought flying over' and the philosophies of consciousness that consider it as both possible and praiseworthy. He does his best to render thought enigmatic by showing its roots in perception. The philosopher's thinking, which Husserl said is forever beginning, is a thinking about the beginning. It tells us that no thought can be liberated absolutely from this beginning, for mind is grounded in eye. What remains then, is for the *cogito* to declare itself and proclaim its rights, as well as a science to be elaborated and a human order instituted. Man forgets that he was born and that he belongs to what gives birth to him. One must therefore mention the mind even if it is only carnal and savage, even if in order to think, it is necessary to be and this being is always a being in the world, a seer-visible (*voyant-visible*).

There remains a final question still concerning the title: eye, of course, but why not ear or hand for that matter? We have found in Merleau-Ponty the idea of a primitive logos, a system of equivalence between elements of the visible. But this system of equivalence is also constituted between diverse sensorial registers, as *The Phenomenology* already stated. Synesthesias are the fate of all perception. Flesh is polymorphous and polyvalent. The sensuous must also allow itself pluralisation, for no matter how subtle the discourse of 'hyperreflection' may be, it can only divulge originary being as having already burst forth. The language it organizes already designates a constituted world where the body has organs and where the perceived is reduced to distinct objects. In order to keep close to this savage logos, should Merleau-Ponty have written "the sensuous and mind?" In any case what *Eye and Mind* says about the visible can also be said of the sonorous and the tactile because it is linked to them. But it seems that Merleau-Ponty wanted to bestow a radical privilege upon the visible. If he evokes music, it is in order to leave it aside. "It doesn't depict anything but certain outlines (épures) of being" (p. 195). As for the tactile, he excludes it from painting. When the young Berenson spoke, a propos of Italian painting, of an evocation of tactile values (and he wasn't the only one), he couldn't have been more mistaken. Painting evokes nothing, least of all the tactile" (p. 200). But in the absence of evocations, there are equivalences attesting that the whole body is solicited. It is on this condition that the tactile makes itself visible. Vision is not devouring, it is mobilizing.

It still remains that the eye is, for what Descartes called the practice of life, the most important organ. Here one has no need to invoke the symbolism with which psychoanalysis burdens it! I would willingly say that if Merleau-Ponty chose to write *Eye and Mind*, it is simply because he loved painting. Others will say that his desire was invested in paintings rather than in music. And after all, that is not such a bad investment!

Translated by Dennis J. Gallagher